AWS Certified Solution Architect - Associate

Practice Questions
Version 1

www.ipspecialist.net

Document Control

Proposal Name	:	AWS – Solution Architect – Practice Questions
Document Version	:	1.0
Document Release Date	:	15th-Sep-2018
Reference	:	SAA-C01

Feedback:

If you have any comments regarding the quality of this book, or otherwise alter it to better suit your needs, you can contact us through email at info@ipspecialist.net

Please make sure to include the book title and ISBN in your message

About IPSpecialist

IPSPECIALIST LTD. IS COMMITTED TO EXCELLENCE AND DEDICATED TO YOUR SUCCESS.

Our philosophy is to treat our customers like family. We want you to succeed, and we are willing to do anything possible to help you make it happen. We have the proof to back up our claims. We strive to accelerate billions of careers with great courses, accessibility, and affordability. We believe that continuous learning and knowledge evolution are most important things to keep re-skilling and up-skilling the world.

Planning and creating a specific goal is where IPSpecialist helps. We can create a career track that suits your visions as well as develop the competencies you need to become a professional Network Engineer. We can also assist you with the execution and evaluation of proficiency level based on the career track you choose, as they are customized to fit your specific goals.

We help you STAND OUT from the crowd through our detailed IP training content packages.

Course Features:

❖ Self-Paced learning
  • Learn at your own pace and in your own time
❖ Covers Complete Exam Blueprint
  • Prep-up for the exam with confidence
❖ Case Study Based Learning
  • Relate the content with real life scenarios
❖ Subscriptions that suits you
  • Get more pay less with IPS Subscriptions
❖ Career Advisory Services
  • Let industry experts plan your career journey
❖ Virtual Labs to test your skills
  • With IPS vRacks, you can testify your exam preparations
❖ Practice Questions
  • Practice Questions to measure your preparation standards
❖ On Request Digital Certification
  • On request digital certification from IPSpecialist LTD

About the Authors:

This book has been compiled with the help of multiple professional engineers. These engineers specialize in different fields e.g Networking, Security, Cloud, Big Data, IoT etc. Each engineer develops content in its specialized field that is compiled to form a comprehensive certification guide.

About the Technical Reviewers:

Nouman Ahmed Khan

AWS-Architect, CCDE, CCIEX5 (R&S, SP, Security, DC, Wireless), CISSP, CISA, CISM is a Solution Architect working with a major telecommunication provider in Qatar. He works with enterprises, mega-projects, and service providers to help them select the best-fit technology solutions. He also works closely as a consultant to understand customer business processes and helps select an appropriate technology strategy to support business goals. He has more than 14 years of experience working in Pakistan/Middle-East & UK. He holds a Bachelor of Engineering Degree from NED University, Pakistan, and M.Sc. in Computer Networks from the UK.

Abubakar Saeed

Abubakar Saeed has more than twenty-five years of experience, Managing, Consulting, Designing, and implementing large-scale technology projects, extensive experience heading ISP operations, solutions integration, heading Product Development, Presales, and Solution Design. Emphasizing on adhering to Project timelines and delivering as per customer expectations, he always leads the project in the right direction with his innovative ideas and excellent management.

Syed Hanif Wasti

Syed Hanif Wasti is a Computer science graduate working professionally as a Technical Content Developer. He is a part of a team of professionals operating in the E-learning and digital education sector. He holds a bachelor's degree in Computer Sciences from PAF-KIET, Pakistan. He has completed training of MCP and CCNA. He has both technical knowledge and industry sounding information, which he uses efficiently in his career. He was working as a Database and Network administrator while having experience of software development.

Areeba Tanveer

Areeba Tanveer is working professionally as a Technical Content Developer. She holds Bachelor's of Engineering degree in Telecommunication Engineering from NED University of Engineering and Technology. She also worked as a project Engineer in Pakistan Telecommunication Company Limited (PTCL). She has both technical knowledge and industry sounding information, which she uses effectively in her career.

Uzair Ahmed

Uzair Ahmed is a professional technical content writer holding bachelor's degree in Computer Science from PAF-KIET university. He has sound knowledge and industry experience in SIEM implementation, .NET development, machine learning, Artificial intelligence, Python programming and other programming and development platforms like React.JS Angular JS Laravel.

Muhammad Yousuf

Muhammad Yousuf is a professional technical content writer. He is Cisco Certified Network Associate in Routing and Switching, holding bachelor's degree in Telecommunication Engineering from Sir Syed University of Engineering and Technology. He has both technical knowledge and industry sounding information, which he uses perfectly in his career.

Free Resources:

With each workbook you buy from Amazon, IPSpecialist offers free resources to our valuable customers.

Once you buy this book you will have to contact us at info@ipspecialist.net or tweet @ipspecialistnet to get this limited time offer without any extra charges.

Free Resources Include:

Exam Practice Questions in Quiz Simulation: IP Specialists' Practice Questions have been developed keeping in mind the certification exam perspective. The collection of these questions from our technology workbooks is prepared to keep the exam blueprint in mind covering not only important but necessary topics as well. It is an ideal document to practice and revise your certification.

Career Report: This report is a step by step guide for a novice who wants to develop his/her career in the field of computer networks. It answers the following queries:

- Current scenarios and future prospects.
- Is this industry moving towards saturation or are new opportunities knocking at the door?
- What will the monetary benefits be?
- Why to get certified?
- How to plan and when will I complete the certifications if I start today?
- Is there any career track that I can follow to accomplish specialization level?

Furthermore, this guide provides a comprehensive career path towards being a specialist in the field of networking and also highlights the tracks needed to obtain certification.

Our Products

Technology Workbooks

IPSpecialist Technology workbooks are the ideal guides to developing the hands-on skills necessary to pass the exam. Our workbook covers official exam blueprint and explains the technology with real life case study based labs. The content covered in each workbook consists of individually focused technology topics presented in an easy-to-follow, goal-oriented, step-by-step approach. Every scenario features detailed breakdowns and thorough verifications to help you completely understand the task and associated technology.

We extensively used mind maps in our workbooks to visually explain the technology. Our workbooks have become a widely used tool to learn and remember the information effectively.

vRacks

Our highly scalable and innovative virtualized lab platforms let you practice the IP Specialist Technology Workbook at your own time and your own place as per your convenience.

Quick Reference Sheets

Our quick reference sheets are a concise bundling of condensed notes of the complete exam blueprint. It's an ideal handy document to help you remember the most important technology concepts related to certification exam.

Practice Questions

IP Specialists' Practice Questions are dedicatedly designed for certification exam perspective. The collection of these questions from our technology workbooks are prepared to keep the exam blueprint in mind covering not only important but necessary topics as well. It's an ideal document to practice and revise your certification.

Become an author & earn with us

If you are interested in becoming an author & want to earn with one time effort. IPS Offers "Earn with us" program for authors & students who have insights on IT related content & want to expand their reach globally can apply for the program here: www.ipspecialist.net/ews

AWS Certifications

AWS Certifications are industry-recognized credentials that validate your technical cloud skills and expertise while assisting in your career growth. These are one of the most valuable IT certifications right now since AWS has established an overwhelming lead in the public cloud market. Even with the presence of several tough competitors such as Microsoft Azure, Google Cloud Engine, and Rackspace, AWS is by far the dominant public cloud platform today, with an astounding collection of proprietary services that continues to grow.

The two key reasons as to why AWS certifications are prevailing in the current cloud-oriented job market:

- There's a dire need for skilled cloud engineers, developers, and architects – and the current shortage of experts is expected to continue into the foreseeable future.
- AWS certifications stand out for their thoroughness, rigor, consistency, and appropriateness for critical cloud engineering positions.

Value of AWS Certifications

AWS places equal emphasis on sound conceptual knowledge of its entire platform, as well as on hands-on experience with the AWS infrastructure and its many unique and complex components and services.

For Individuals

- Demonstrate your expertise to design, deploy, and operate highly available, cost-effective, and secure applications on AWS.
- Gain recognition and visibility for your proven skills and proficiency with AWS.
- Earn tangible benefits such as access to the AWS Certified LinkedIn Community, invite to AWS Certification Appreciation Receptions and Lounges, AWS Certification Practice Exam Voucher, Digital Badge for certification validation, AWS Certified Logo usage, access to AWS Certified Store.
- Foster credibility with your employer and peers.

For Employers

- Identify skilled professionals to lead IT initiatives with AWS technologies.
- Reduce risks and costs to implement your workloads and projects on the AWS platform.

- Increase customer satisfaction.

Types of Certification

Role-Based Certifications:

- *Foundational* - Validates overall understanding of the AWS Cloud. Prerequisite to achieving Specialty certification or an optional start towards Associate certification.
- *Associate* - Technical role-based certifications. No prerequisite.
- *Professional* - Highest level technical role-based certification. Relevant Associate certification required.

Specialty Certifications:

- Validate advanced skills in specific technical areas.
- Require one active role-based certification.

About AWS – Certified Solutions Architect Associate Exam

Exam Questions	Multiple choice and multiple answer
Number of Questions	65
Time to Complete	130 minutes
Available Languages	English, Japanese, Simplified Chinese, Korean
Practice Exam Fee	20 USD
Exam Fee	150 USD

The AWS Certified Solutions Architect – Associate (SAA-C01) examination is intended for individuals who perform a Solutions Architect role. This exam validates an examinee's ability to effectively demonstrate knowledge of how to architect and deploy secure and robust applications on AWS technologies.

It validates an examinee's ability to:

- Define a solution using architectural design principles based on customer requirements.
- Provide implementation guidance based on best practices to the organization throughout the lifecycle of the project.

Recommended AWS Knowledge

- One year of hands-on experience designing available, cost-efficient, fault-tolerant, and scalable distributed systems on AWS
- Hands-on experience using compute, networking, storage, and database AWS services
- Hands-on experience with AWS deployment and management services
- Ability to identify and define technical requirements for an AWS-based application
- Ability to identify which AWS services meet a given technical requirement
- Knowledge of recommended best practices for building secure and reliable applications on the AWS platform
- An understanding of the basic architectural principles of building on the AWS cloud
- An understanding of the AWS global infrastructure
- An understanding of network technologies as they relate to AWS
- An understanding of security features and tools that AWS provides and how they relate to traditional service.

	Domain	%
Domain 1	Design Resilient Architectures	34%
Domain 2	Define Performant Architectures	24%
Domain 3	Specify Secure Applications and Architectures	26%
Domain 4	Design Cost-Optimized Architectures	10%
Domain 5	Define Operationally Excellent Architectures	6%
Total		100%

Practice Questions

1. A solutions architect peered two VPCs (VPC A & VPC B); A as requester and B as accepter. Both the VPCs can communicate with each other. Now, it is required that the resources in both the VPCs can connect to the internet but, anyone on the internet should not be able to reach resources that are inside the VPC. What should be done?

   a) Create a NAT gateway on Requestor VPC, and configure a route in route table with NAT gateway. The acceptor VPC can be routed to the internet through VPC A internet gateway

   b) Create NAT gateways on both VPCs and configure routes in respective route tables with NAT gateways

   c) Create a NAT instance on Requester VPC (VPC A). This NAT instance will route VPC B to the internet

   d) Create an internet gateway on requester VPC and configure a route in route table with internet gateway. VPC B will be routed to the internet by VPC A internet gateway

2. An organization has a VPC (10.10.0.0/16) with two private and one public (10.10.1.0/24) subnets. Private subnet 1 (ps1 - 10.10.2.0/24) and private subnet 2 (ps2 - 10.10.3.0/24). Public subnet has the main route table, and the two private subnets have their route tables. The sysops team reported a problem which stated that the EC2 instance in ps1 is unable to communicate with the RDS MySQL database that is in ps2. Select all possible reasons for this problem.

   a) RDS security group does not contain an outbound rule for all traffic or port 3306

   b) 10.10.3.0/24 subnet's ACL does not have an inbound Allow rule set for all traffic

   c) RDS security group is not correctly configured with 10.10.1.0/24 instead of 10.10.2.0/24

   d) One of the private subnet route table's local route is changed to restrict access only within the subnet IP range

3. As a solutions architect, for an organization, you have setup a VPC with CIDR range 10.10.0.0/16. Created an IGW and new route table, and added a new route with IGW as target and 0.0.0.0/0 as a destination. Also, you have created two subnets, one for public

and the other for private and launched a Linux instance on a public subnet with Auto-assign public IP option enabled. After all this effort, when you tried to SSH the new machine, the connection got failed. What could be the reason?

    a) The public IP address is not assigned
    b) Elastic IP is not assigned
    c) Both the subnets are associated with the main route table; no subnet is explicitly attached with new route table that has the IGW route.
    d) None of the above

4. Your company wants to upload files to S3 bucket privately through VPC. In your existing VPC, you already have a subnet and route table that contains a route to the NAT gateway. To fulfil the new requirement, you created VPC Endpoint for S3 and added same route table. Unfortunately, in the S3 server logs, you found out that the requests to S3 from an EC2 instance within the subnet that you have associated with the mentioned route table are going to the internet through the NAT gateway. What is the possible reason?

    a) S3 is a managed service; all requests will always go through the internet
    b) S3 bucket is in a different region than the VPC
    c) The EC2 instance has an EIP associated with it
    d) When NAT gateway and VPC Endpoint exist on same route table, the NAT gateway always takes precedence

5. An organization has a VPC with S3 VPC Endpoint that serves some S3 buckets. You were asked to create a new S3 bucket and reuse the existing VPC Endpoint to route requests to the new bucket. You performed the task, and then you found that the requests are failing with an "Access Denied" error. Select 2 reasons for this problem.

    a) You need to add new S3 bucket host name as destination and VPC Endpoint ID as a target in the route table
    b) AWS default deny policy restricting access to IAM user who already has access to S3 bucket
    c) AWS IAM role/user does not have access to the new S3 bucket

d) VPV Endpoint contains a policy, currently restricted to many S3 buckets and does not contain the new one

6. You want to download patches on an EC2 instance which resides in a private subnet inside a custom VPC. You created a NAT gateway and added a route to the route table. However, the connection getting timed-out when you are trying to download patches on the EC2 instance. Select 2 reasons for this issue.

   a) The inbound rules of the NAT gateway's security group do not allow traffic from EC2 instance
   b) Security group's outbound rules for EC2 instance are restricted to allow internet traffic
   c) NAT gateway is created without an EIP
   d) NAT gateway created in private subnet without an internet gateway

7. You have been assigned with a task to build a solution for a web application that contains a web server and an RDS instance. The existing environment has a VPC with a private subnet and public subnet which has a route to the internet through an IGW. Provide the best and cost-efficient solution.

   a) Web server EC2 in public subnet with Elastic IP, RDS in private subnet
   b) A Bastion-host in public subnet, web server EC2 in private subnet with NAT gateway, RDS also in private subnet
   c) A Bastion-host in public, web server EC2 with EIP in public subnet, and RDS in private subnet
   d) A Bastion-host in public subnet, web server EC2 and RDS instance in private subnets

8. You are asked to build a group of EC2 Linux instances in your AWS environment to handle scheduled heavy workloads and write the data into AWS RedShift. All the stakeholders need to login to these instances to develop, fix and deploy workloads only within the organization's network. Provide a secure and cost-effective solution.

   a) AWS VPN connection from your organization to AWS VPC, EC2 instances in a VPN enabled subnet with secure SSH keys to login, RedShift in private subnet

b) VPN connection from your organization to VPC, Bastion-host in VPN enabled subnet with secure SSH keys to login, EC2 instances in private subnet with secure SSH keys to login, RedShift I private subnet

c) A Bastion-host in public subnet with secure SSH key to login, EC2 instances in private subnet with secure SSH keys to login, RedShift in private subnet

d) EC2 instances on a public subnet with secure SSH keys to login, RedShift in private subnet

9. You have a Bastion-host EC2 instance on a VPC public subnet. Assuming that the route table is setup with internet gateway, what would be the minimal configuration that is required to for SSH request to work?

a) Allow port 22 and SSH protocol on security group inbound, network ACL inbound, network ACL outbound for your IP address

b) Allow port 22 and SSH protocol on security group inbound, network ACL inbound for your IP address

c) Allow port 22 and SSH protocol on security group inbound and outbound, network ACL inbound for your IP address

d) Allow port 22 and SSH protocol on security group inbound and outbound, network ACL inbound, network ACL outbound for IP range 0.0.0.0/0

10. Below are given Network ACL and Security Group rules. Evaluate these rules and find out what would happen to an SSH request sent from IP address 10.10.1.148 to an EC2 instance with below security group and exists inside a subnet with below Network ACL rules?

NACL Inbound

Rule #	Type	Protocol	Port Range	Source	Allow/Deny
100	SSH (22)	TCP (6)	22	10.10.1.0/24	Allow
200	SSH (22)	TCP (6)	22	10.10.1.148/32	Deny
300	All traffic	All	All	10.10.1.248/31	Allow
*	All traffic	All	All	0.0.0.0/0	Deny

NACL Outbound

Rule#	Type	Protocol	Port Range	Source	Allow/Deny
100	All traffic	All	All	0.0.0.0/0	Allow
*	All traffic	ALL	ALL	0.0.0.0/0	Deny

Security Group Inbound

Type	Protocol	Port Range	Source	Description
SSH (22)	TCP (6)	22	10.10.1.0/24	

Security Group Outbound

Type	Protocol	Port Range	Source	Description
SSH (22)	TCP (6)	22	172.32.1.0/24	

 a) SSH request fails due to security group outbound rule does not allow 10.10.1.148 IP address
 b) SSH request fails due to rule # 200 in NACL inbound rule
 c) SSH request succeeds due to rule # 300 in NACL inbound and rule # 100 in NACL outbound, security group inbound rule
 d) SSH request succeeds due to rule # 100 in NACL inbound and outbound, security group inbound rule

11. Following are Network ACL rules defined in your subnet which is associated with a route table having an internet gateway

Inbound Rules

Rule #	Type	Protocol	Port Range	Source	Allow/Deny
100	All traffic	All	All	0.0.0.0/0	Allow

| 200 | SSH (22) | TCP (6) | 22 | 0.0.0.0/0 | Deny |
| * | All traffic | All | All | 0.0.0.0/0 | Deny |

Outbound Rules

Rule #	Type	Protocol	Port Range	Source	Allow/Deny
100	SSH (22)	TCP(6)	22	0.0.0.0/0	Deny
200	All traffic	All	All	0.0.0.0/0	Allow
*	All traffic	All	All	0.0.0.0/0	Deny

What will happen when an SSH request is made to an EC2 instance with a pubic IP address inside this subnet?

 a) SSH request will fail due to outbound rule # 100
 b) SSH request will be successful because of inbound rule # 100
 c) SSH request will fail because of the * rule; Deny all traffic
 d) SSH request will fail due to specific deny for SSH traffic

12. Evaluate the following ACL rules and select the correct statement for the case of a request that is originated from IP address 10.10.1.148.

Inbound Rules

Rule #	Type	Protocol	Port Range	Source	Allow/Deny
100	HTTPS (443)	TCP (6)	443	0.0.0.0/0	Allow
200	SSH (22)	TCP (6)	22	10.10.148/32	Deny
300	All traffic	All	All	10.10.1.0/24	Allow
400	SSH (22)	TCP (6)	22	10.10.0.0/16	Deny

*	All traffic	All	All	0.0.0.0/0	Deny

Outbound Rules

Rule #	Type	Protocol	Port Range	Destination	Allow/Deny
100	SSH (22)	TCP (6)	22	0.0.0.0/0	Allow
200	HTTPS (443)	TCP (6)	443	10.10.1.0/24	Allow
*	All traffic	All	All	0.0.0.0/0	Deny

Please Select:
a) All requests except HTTPS (443) will fail
b) HTTP (80) request will succeed
c) SSH (22) requests will succeed
d) HTTPS (443) request will succeed

13. As an architect, your task is to transfer the data to S3 without going to the internet to comply with the security policies. Your network is connected to VPC through VPN, and the VPC contains S3 VPC gateway endpoint to access S3 through AWS internal network. The data to be transferred is on the organization's network. Suggest the best possible method to get the required task done.

a) Add a new route in VPC's VPN enabled route table with VPC endpoint to support direct transfer from the remote network to S3
b) Create VPN gateway endpoint to support this use case
c) VPC gateway endpoint can be used with organization's network, and data can be privately sent to S3 from a remote network
d) Setup an S3 proxy on EC2 instance within VPC and transfer data through VPN and S3 proxy to S3

14. You have a VPC in your nearest AWS region, you have created VPC endpoint for S3 and added it to the main route table. You also upgraded your EC2 instance that is inside a subnet which is associated to the main route table. When requests generated to S3 from

the upgraded instance, the connection got failed. The S3 bucket is in the same region. Select all possible regions for this issue.

a) Main route table does not have NAT gateway association
b) Subnet's NACL inbound rules do not allow traffic from S3
c) Main route table does not have internet gateway association
d) EC2 instance security group outbound rules are restricted and do not contain prefix list

15. You have created three VPCs (A, B & C) and peered these three; A to B and B to C. You created a NAT gateway in VPC B and tried to use the same NAT gateway for resources that are inside VPCs A and C. You found out that, resources within A & C cannot communicate to internet through the NAT gateway, but resources inside B are communicating. Select the possible reason.

a) NAT gateway is not created inside VPC B's public subnet
b) VPC B's subnet which contains NAT gateway is not configured in VPC A and VPC C route tables
c) Using another VPC NAT gateway is not supported in AWS
d) Route tables in VPC A and VPC C are not configured to use VPC B's NAT gateway

16. You have launched EC2 instances in two VPCs that are peered and tried to communicate through peering connection. From the given options, select the reason for request getting timed out.

a) Route tables of both VPCs only contain specific IP range for peering connection
b) Peered VPCs are in different regions
c) NACLs have been configured not to allow traffic from peered VPC
d) Security groups of EC2 instances are not configured to allow traffic from peered VPC

17. A trainee architect complained that he created a VPC with CIDR range 10.10.0.0/16 and a subnet with CIDR range 10.10.1.0/24. When he went to the VPC console subnets and looked at the newly created subnet, he could only find 251 IP addresses although /24

CIDR comes with 256 addresses. He hasn't launched any resources in the VPC. What could be the reason behind this?

a) AWS launches monitoring resources in new VPCs
b) AWS reserves 5 IP addresses for every VPC and selects these five addresses from the first subnet
c) AWS reserves 5 IP addresses of every subnet
d) None of the above

18. You are asked to setup a VPC and a private subnet, also a VPN connection with your company to communicate with the resources within the VPC. Your organization may require DNS names for some on-premise apps to communicate with VPC. You launched a new EC2 instance with the auto-assign public as disable but when the instance got ready, you notice that Public DNS name is missing, what will you do?

a) You cannot have private DNS names for custom VPCs
b) Set auto-assign public IP to use subnet settings
c) Enable DNS resolution for VPC
d) Enable DNS hostnames for VPC

19. You are asked to build a new application that requires a combination of 20 EC2 instances. These instances should be kept inside a private VPC in a manner that the instances could communicate with each other, and receive requests from all other EC2 instances within the VPC, without receiving any traffic from the internet. The existing VPC is created with 10.10.0.0/24 CIDR range (256 IP addresses). All of these 256 addresses are consumed by eight subnets with /27 CIDR ranges. How would the newly required architecture be built?

a) Launch EC2 instances in different subnets and setup security groups and ACLs to allow traffic between EC2 instances
b) Edit subnet CIDR ranges to /28 and free up unused IP addresses
c) Add secondary CIDR range for the VPC, create new subnet and setup all instances in the same subnet
d) Create a new VPC and setup 20 EC2 instances in it. Peer the new VPC with the old one

20. You have setup two VPCs A and B with 10.10.0.0/16 and 10.11.0.0/16 respectively with a VPC peering connection. Select the correct route table configuration from the given options to make VPC peering work.

    a) VPC A route table contains route with destination as 10.10.1.0/24, and VPC B route table contains route with destination as 10.11.1.0/28
    b) VPC B route table contains route with destination as 10.10.1.0/24, and VPC A contains route with destination as 10.11.1.0/28
    c) VPC A route table contains route with destination as 10.11.0.0/16
    d) VPC B route table contains route with destination as 10.10.0.0/16

21. You have joined an organization, and you are facing this, a VPC setup with 40 routes for different purposes such as VPC peering, VPN connections, NAT gateways with different IP ranges. The IP range for the VPC is 10.10.0.0/16, and a number of teams are working on the VPC to create subnets for their applications that need to have custom route tables. The application custom route tables are associated with the main route table which also has an Internet gateway to act for the public subnet. For all that, at many times, teams forget to explicitly associate the custom route table to the subnets. This will implicitly associate with main route table that has the IGW which causes security concerns. When connections do not work as expected, it takes a lot of time to troubleshoot. You are asked to resolve this issue, select the solution from the following

    a) Delete all routes from the custom table and add to the main route table. Delete all routes from the main table and add to the custom table
    b) Delete internet gateway from the main route table
    c) Make a custom route table as main route table. New subnets created will now simply associate with it
    d) Create a script to create subnet and associate new subnet with a custom route table

22. As a solutions architect, how will you solve this issue?
    An application team in your organization came to you and stated that requests from an EC2 instance to an RDS in the same VPC are successful but getting timed out when sent to another subnet. Claiming that the connections were working before.

a) Check OS level logs inside EC2 instance
b) Check OS level logs inside RDS instance
c) Check CloudWatch Metrics for RDS instance
d) Create VPC flow log for subnet where RDS instance is launched

23. Following are security group inbound rules.

Type	Protocol	Port Range	Source
HTTP (80)	TCP (6)	80	10.10.1.148/32
HTTP (80)	TCP (6)	80	10.10.1.0/28
All TCP	TCP (6)	All	10.10.1.148/32
SSH (22)	TCP (6)	22	10.10.1.0/28
Custom UDP	UDP (17)	3000	10.10.1.148/32

Evaluate these rules and select the correct statement

a) Custom UDP rule port 3000 for source 10.10.1.148/32 is duplicated
b) SSH port 22 for source 10.10.1.0/28 is duplicated
c) HTTP port 80 for source 10.10.1.148/32 is duplicated
d) All rules are correct

24. Following is a route table configuration

Destination	Target	Status	Propagated
30.0.0.0/20	Local	Active	No
20.0.0.0/16	Local	Active	No

This route table was initially created with 20.0.0.0/16. Which of the following statement is correct?

a) Secondary IP CIDR range 30.0.0.0/20 for VPC with local route
b) DirectConnect connection route for remote network with 30.0.0.0/20 IP range
c) VPN connection route for a remote network with 30.0.0.0/20 IP range

d) VPC peering connection route for VPC with 30.0.0.0/20 IP range

25. You setup a VPC for your company with CIDR range 10.10.0.0/16. Multiple application teams use different subnets, and there are a total of 100 subnets being actively used. One of these teams who is using 50 EC2 instances in subnet 10.10.55.0/24 complains that they are facing network connection failures for almost 30 EC2 instances in any given period. What will you do to overcome this issue with minimal configuration and minimal logs written?

a) Create a flow log for subnet 10.10.55.0/24
b) Create flow log for each EC2 instance network interface one by one and troubleshoot the connections issue
c) Create a flow log for the VPC and filter the logs in CloudWatch log group
d) None of the above

26. An S3 bucket is created in the region, us-east-1. The default "configure options" and "permissions" were not changed. Select the options that are not included in the default settings?

a) Versioning is enabled
b) No bucket policy exists
c) Transfer acceleration is enabled
d) Encryption is enabled

27. Which of the following are S3 bucket properties?

a) Metadata
b) Storage class
c) Object level logging
d) Server access logging

28. You created an S3 bucket in sa-east-1(Sao Paolo) while you are in the Asia Pacific. You kept the default settings for the bucket and deleted some objects by using AWS CLI. Still, when you tried to list the objects in the bucket, you still see the objects that you

have deleted. You are even able to download those objects. What could be the reason for this?

a) AWS provides strong consistency for DELETES
b) AWS keeps a copy of deleted objects for seven days in standard storage
c) AWS provides eventual consistency for DELETES
d) AWS does not support cross-region DELETES

29. You are asked to upload a large number of files to the cloud. These files should be immediately available across different geographical locations right after the upload is done. What will you do?

a) S3 is suitable for immediate downloads because AWS provides strong consistency for new objects
b) EFS is suitable for immediate downloads because AWS provides eventual consistency for new objects
c) S3 is suitable for immediate downloads because AWS provides Read-After-Write consistency
d) S3 is not suitable for immediate downloads because AWS provides eventual consistency for new objects

30. You are building an on-premise application and want the storage on AWS. Data must only be accessed via the application because there are relational logics in the application. Administrators should be able to access the data directly from AWS S3 console, bypassing the application. Select the best solution

a) Custom built S3 solution
b) File gateway
c) Stored volume gateway
d) Cached volume gateway

31. You have created an S3 bucket in us-east-1 region with default configuration. You have uploaded some documents and wanted to share it with a group of users in your organization. What will you do?

a) By default, the S3 bucket has public access enabled, share the document's URL with users via email

b) Generate pre-signed URL with an expiry date and share the URL with all persons via email

c) Create one IAM user per person, add them to an IAM group, attach managed policy for the group with GetObject action on your S3 bucket. Users can download documents from the AWS console

d) Create one IAM user per person, attach managed policy for each user with GetObject action on your S3 bucket. Users can login to AWS console and download documents

32. Which of the following are valid statements for Amazon S3? Choose multiple options

a) S3 provides eventual consistency for overwrite PUTS and DELETES

b) S3 might return prior data when a process replaces an existing object and immediately attempts to read

c) A successful response to a PUT request for a new object only occurs when the object is completely saved

d) S3 provides strong consistency for PUTS and DELETES

e) S3 provides read-after-write consistency for any type of PUTS

33. You are asked to design a web application which stores static assets in a S3 bucket. The expected number of requests that could include Get Put and Delete is 6000. What will you do to make sure that the performance remains optimal?

a) Use multi-part upload

b) Add a random prefix to the key names

c) Amazon S3 will automatically manage performance at this scale

d) Use a predictable naming scheme, such as sequential numbers or date-time sequences in the key names

34. You have an application running on EC2; when it tried to upload a 7 GB file to S3, the operation got failed. Select the reason and solution for this problem

a) VPC endpoints only support data transfers up to 5 GB. Use EBS optimized instance

b) NAT gateway only supports data transfers up to 5 GB. Use EBS provisioned IOPS and use an Amazon EBS optimized instance

c) EC2 is designed to work best with EBS volumes. Use EBS provisioned IOPS and use an Amazon EBS optimized instance

d) With a single PUT operation, you can upload objects up to 5 GB. Use multi-part upload for larger file uploads

35. You have launched an EC2 instance with a role that has GetObject permissions on the S3 bucket defined in its policy. An application is running on EC2 that stores the files in an S3 bucket. Authenticated users get pre-signed URLs for the files in the S3 bucket using EC2 role temporary credentials. After all that, users report that they get an error when accessing pre-signed URLs. What could be the reason? Select 2

a) Default policy on temporary credentials does not have GetObject privileges on S3 bucket

b) The bucket might have a policy with deny, and EC2 role is not whitelisted.

c) Logged in user must be an IAM user to download the file through pre-signed URLs

d) Pre-signed URLs expired

36. Your organization stores confidential information in an S3 bucket, access is granted to some programmatic IAM users. These IAM users are restricted to generate requests inside your organization's IP address range. In spite of that, it is noticed that there are requests from other IP addresses to download objects from S3 buckets. How will you find out the requester IP address?

a) Enable CloudWatch metrics

b) Enable CloudTrail logging using OPTIONS object

c) Enable server logging

d) Enable VPC flow logs in the region where S3 bucket exists

37. An idea of web and mobile application is presented to you, these apps can upload 100,000 images into S3, and a sudden increase in volume is expected. As an architect,

you are asked for a cost-effective solution. Is S3 suitable for this requirement? What information do you need to gather to make a decision? Choose 2

a) Information of total size to properly design prefix namespace
b) Information of total size to provision storage on S3 bucket
c) Information of number of requests during peak time
d) Information of high availability of data and frequency of requests to choose storage class of objects in S3

38. Which of the following are system metadata for objects in S3? (Choose 3)

a) x – amz – meta – location
b) Content – length
c) x – amz – version – id
d) x – amz – meta – object – id
e) x – amz – server – side – encryption

39. Your organization is going through an audit, and it needs to log all the requests sent to a group of 10 buckets. The data stored in the bucket is confidential, and it is required to meet compliance. The logs will also be used to check if any requests are coming outside the organization's IP address range. Your application team enabled S3 server access logging for all the buckets into a common logging bucket named s3-server-logging. After a few hours, they are noticing that no logs have been written to the logging bucket. What could be the reason?

a) Bucket name for server access logging should be s3-server-access-logging to write the request logs
b) Write access is disabled for log delivery group
c) Bucket public access is not enabled
d) Bucket user defined policy is not allowing log delivery group write into an S3 bucket

40. You build a web application for your organization where authenticated users can upload videos. These videos were to be stored in an S3 bucket. When you tested the application,

you come to know that the requests to S3 are being blocked. What will you do to make the upload work?

a) Web application URL must be added to bucket policy to allow PutObject requests
b) Add content-length and content-MD5 headers while sending upload requests to S3
c) Add configuration in S3 bucket CORS to allow PUT requests from web application URL
d) Enable public access to allow uploads from web applications

41. You uploaded a file with content 'name' to your S3 bucket. Then you overwrite the file with content 'phone'. You generate a GetObject request right after overwrite. What output are you expecting?

a) An error: "object updating. Please try after some time."
b) Either 'name' or 'phone' or no result
c) Phone
d) Name

42. You created a bucket named "mybucket" in US west region. What are the valid URLs for accessing the bucket? (Choose multiple)

a) https://s3.amazonaws.com/mybucket
b) https://s3.us-west-1.amazonaws.com/mybucket
c) https://s3-us-west-1.amazonaws.com/mybucket
d) https://s3.mybucket.us-west-1.amazonaws.com
e) https://mybucket.s3-us-west-1.amazonaws.com

43. Select the minimum and maximum file sizes that can be stored to Amazon S3

a) 0 bytes and 5 Terra-Bytes
b) 1 byte and 5 Giga-Bytes
c) 1 KB and 5 Terra-Bytes
d) 1 KB and 5 Giga-Bytes

44. Lots of application logs are written on an S3 bucket regularly. These are the only copies and are not replicated anywhere. The log files range between 10MB to 500MB in size and are not required frequently. To troubleshoot application issues, logs are required, and this happens once in a while. You are asked to make 60 days log available immediately when required, the record older than 60 days should be kept but is required only for reference, not on a regular basis. What solution do you have to keep the billing cost minimum?

   a) Set object storage class to OneZone-IA. Use lifecycle management to move data from OneZone-IA to Glacier after 60 days
   b) Set storage class to Standard. Use lifecycle management to move data from Standard to Standard-IA after 30 days and move data from Standard-IA to Glacier after 30 days
   c) Set object storage class to Standard. Move data from Standard to Standard-IA after 60 days
   d) Set object storage class to Standard-IA. Use lifecycle management to move data from Standard-IA to Glacier after 60 days

45. You created a bucket 25 days ago, on the day you created this bucket; you uploaded a 1GB file. On day 15, you uploaded 5GB data to the same bucket. You also enabled versioning on this bucket. How will billing be applied to this scenario?

   a) Charges 5 GB for 25 days
   b) Charges 1 GB for 14 days and 5 GB for 11 days
   c) Charges 1 GB for 25 days 5 GB for 11 days
   d) Charges 6 GB for 25 days

46. You have one versioning enabled S3 bucket. You accidentally deleted an object that has three versions. What will you do to restore the deleted object?

   a) In version-enabled bucket, DELETE request only deletes the latest version.
   b) Versioning does not support the restoration of deleted objects
   c) Delete the delete marker on the object
   d) Select the deleted object and click restore option in More menu

47. Your application writes its logs to a version-enabled S3 bucket. Each object has multiple versions. The app deletes the objects from the bucket through Delete API after 60 days. After all this, in the next month's bill, you are charged for S3 usage. Why?

    a) Delete API for all versions of the object in version-enabled bucket cannot be done through API. It can only be done by the owner from the console
    b) Delete API call moves the object with its versions to S3 recycle bin
    c) Delete API call does not delete the actual object but only places a delete marker on it
    d) Delete API call only deletes the latest version

48. You have an application on EC2 which is uploading objects of sizes 10-20 GB by using multi-part upload to an S3 bucket. You want to notify a group of people that the upload is completed, but these people do not have IAM accounts. How will you notify them? (Choose 2)

    a) Write a custom script on your app to poll S3 bucket for new files and send emails through SES sandbox
    b) Write a custom script on your app to poll S3 bucket for new files and send emails through SES non-sandbox
    c) Use S3 event notification and configure SNS which sends email to the subscribed email address
    d) Use S3 event function and configure Lambda function which sends email using SES non-sandbox

49. An S3 bucket in us-east-1 is used to store video files for a video sharing website that is running on EC2 inside the US. The owners have decided to expand the website all over the world. After the expansion, customers from outside the US region started complaining that the upload, download and overall access to the web are very slow. You are hired to resolve this issue; what solution do you have?

    a) Change your app design to provision higher memory configuration EC2 instances and process S3 requests through EC2

b) Enable transfer acceleration feature of S3 that improves upload and download speed by using edge locations
c) Use VPC endpoints in other regions to improve S3 uploads and downloads
d) Use CloudFront for improving the performance by caching static files on the website

50. Is it necessary to enable versioning for cross-region replication?

a) Yes, on both source and destination buckets
b) Only on source bucket
c) Only on destination bucket
d) Versioning is useful to avoid accidental deletes and not a requirement for cross-region replication

51. For a newly created security group, to allow SSH to connect to instances and communication between EC2 and EFS. Which of the following statements is correct?

a) Open port 111 (NFS) on EC2 security group and ports 111 (NFS) and 2049 (NFS) on EFS security group
b) Open port 2049 (NFS) on EC2 security group and ports 111 (NFS) and 2049 (NFS) on EFS security group
c) Open port 22 (SSH) on EC2 security group and ports 111 (NFS) and 2049 (NFS) on EFS security group
d) Open port 22 (SSH) on EC2 security group and port 2049 (NFS) on EFS security group

52. Which of the following are characteristics of EFS? (Choose 2)

a) Cross region replication
b) Big data and analytics, media processing workflows, content management, web serving, and home directories
c) Boot volumes, transactional and NoSQL databases, data warehousing and ETL
d) Data is stored redundantly in a single AZ
e) Up to thousands of EC2 instances, from multiple AZs, can connect concurrently to a file system

53. On an EC2 instance, you mounted EFS with default settings. Now, you are asked to encrypt data during transit to comply with regulatory policies. How can encryption be enabled during transit?

    a) Enable encryption during mounting on EC2 using Amazon EFS mount helper. Unmount un-encrypted mount and remount using mount helper encryption during transit option.

    b) Encryption during transit can only be enabled during EFS creation. You need to create encryption during transit EFS, copy data from old EFS to new EFS and delete the old one

    c) Edit EFS to enable "encryption during transit" setting

    d) EFS uses NFS protocol which encrypts the data in transit by default

54. Due to regulatory policies, your organization has asked you to encrypt the data that is stored on EFS, which is mounted on an EC2 instance with default settings. How will you enable encryption?

    a) EFS does not support encryption, Use S3 instead

    b) You can enable encryption at rest during mounting of EFS on EC2

    c) You will create encryption-at-rest EFS, copy data from old EFS to new EFS and delete the old one

    d) Edit EFS volume and enable "Encryption-at-rest" setting

55. Your organization's existing VPC is in us-east-1 having two subnets in us-east-1b. EC2 instances are running in both subnets. These instances require a common file store to share files for heavy workloads. You created an EFS and mounted on all instances and enable them to share files across all the instances. Then, you were asked to increase the number of EC2 instances due to increase in load of work. You created a new subnet in us-east-1c and launched few instances. When you tried to mount the previously created EFS on new EC2 instances, operation getting failed. Why?

    a) EFS mount target security group inbound rules does not allow traffic from new EC2 instances

b) EFS created with mount targets in us-east-1b availability zone. Instances in us-east-1c cannot use EFS mount target in us-east-1b

c) By default, EFS is only available in one availability zone. Create a case with AWS support to increase EFS availability zones

d) EFS does not support cross availability zone mounting

56. Your organization has an AWS setup with a VPC in us-east-1 and a fleet of 20 EC2 instances. These instances are attached to EFS with mount targets on all VPC availability zones. You are asked to setup the same environment in another VPC within the same region using same EFS volumes. How will you do this?

a) EFS can be used only within one VPC at a time. You need to launch EC2 instances in existing VPC

b) EFS is available for all VPCs within a region by default. Mount EFS on new EC2 instances and configure EFS security group to allow inbound traffic

c) Peer both VPCs, launch C5 or M5 EC2 instances on new VPC and mount existing EFS on new EC2 instances

d) Attach new VPC to existing EFS, create new mount targets for new VPC and mount EFS on EC2 instances within new VPC

57. VPC A and B are peered together. You created an EFS for VPC A but when tried to mount it on an EC2 instance in VPC B; you got connection timed out. What is the reason? (Choose 3)

a) EFS cannot be mounted through VPC peering

b) VPC B's EC2 instance types are not M5 or C5

c) Security groups on mount targets do not have NFS port open to VPC B's EC2 instance

d) VPC B could be in a different region than VPC A

e) EFS takes up to an hour after creation to make mount targets available

58. You are required to build a web application with 20 load balanced EC2 instances to serve content. Content storage has to be the same for all instances. You have chosen EFS as common storage. You are required to have as low latency as possible when serving content to the users. Choose Solution from the following

a) Performance mode = Max I/O, provides low latency access to EFS
b) Performance mode = Max I/O, provides better performance when sharing EFS across more than 10 EC2 instances
c) Performance mode = General purpose, provides low latency access to EFS
d) Performance mode = General purpose, AWS can handle performance with general purpose mode till 10s of EC2 instances

59. You are building a content serving web application. This app contains 5 EC2 instances with load balancers. Total size of the content stored will not exceed 25 GB. Large number of users access the content frequently. Choose the throughput mode to ensure that the applications on EC2 instances to EFS data transfer will not have low performance?

a) Throughput mode = Provisioned, AWS provisions high throughput for smaller data sizes and vice versa
b) Throughput mode = Provisioned, you can configure specific throughput irrespective of EFS data size
c) Throughput mode = Bursting, automatically bursts throughput based on the requests irrespective of EFS data size
d) Throughput mode = Bursting, provides a consistent high throughput for smaller data sizes

60. For big data analysis, the data is expected to be 400 TB. The analysts are planning to use 150 EC2 instances with EFS to achieve better performance for the analysis. You are asked recommend performance mode. What will be your suggestion?

a) Performance mode = Max I/O, provides higher levels of aggregate throughput and operations per second with a tradeoff of slightly higher latencies
b) Performance mode = General purpose, provides higher level of aggregate throughput and operations per second
c) Performance mode = General purpose, provides low latency access to EFS
d) Performance mode = General purpose, AWS can handle performance with general purpose mode till 10s of EC2 instances

61. Using API gateway, you created a REST API and deployed it on production. You are requested to provide the details of accesses to the API for auditing purpose. How would you get the required information?

    a) Enable logging in your backend system to log the requests
    b) CloudTrail contains the requester information for your API
    c) Enable access logging
    d) Enable CloudWatch logs

62. Your organization needs to expose some services to its customer. Using the AWS API gateway, you created and deployed REST API for your organization over public internet. After that, you noticed that requests are coming from hosts other than your customer. How will you control access?

    a) Generate and distribute client certificate to customer and ask them to use these certificates while sending requests
    b) Create IAM users for your customer
    c) Configure your customer's IP address ranges in resource policy
    d) Enable CORS and add required host names under access control allow origin
    e) Establish DirectConnect to each of your customer's network and enable API gateway's VPC link through a private VPC

63. You created a REST API using API gateway for your organization and exposed it over the internet. Now you are noticing a consistent high number of requests on GET/users method, 5000 out of 9000 are sent in the 1st millisecond approximately. This is causing overload on the backend systems. You changed the stage's number of requests per second to 6000 and burst to 3000 requests. Now, the total number of per second sent requests is reduced to 6000. But still, 5000 requests are being sent at the 1st millisecond. What is the reason of this behavior?

    a) Requests per second are set to 6000. API can serve up to 6000 requests regardless of how many requests sent in one millisecond
    b) Any changes made to stage might take up to 2 hours to propagate
    c) Account level throttle settings are 10000 requests per second and burst 5000 requests. You cannot overwrite account level settings

d) Stage's Get/users method throttle settings might have overwritten stage throttle settings with burst as 5000 requests

64. Using the API gateway, you have built a REST API and distributed to your customers. Still, your API is getting huge amount of requests that is causing performance bottleneck. Eventually, it is causing failures in serving your customers. How can the API performance be improved? (Choose 2)

    a) Enable load balancer on your backend systems
    b) Enable API caching to serve frequently requested data from API cache
    c) Create a resource policy to allow access for specific customers during specific time period
    d) Enable throttling and control the number of requests per second

65. Choose multiple from the following, the valid integration sources for API gateway?

    a) SFTP connection
    b) VPC Link
    c) Database connections on internet outside AWS network
    d) Lambda functions from another account
    e) Public facing HTTPS-based endpoints outside AWS network

66. The XYZ company, has an on premise network where they have some 100s of APIs exposed to the internet. They are integrated with AWS through DirectConnect. Now, they come to know the resilience and reduced cost of AWS API Gateway. You are asked to provide them with a cost effective way to make these REST APIs available through AWS API Gateway. What will be your solution for them?

    a) Build API Gateway with integration type as AWS service and select DirectConnect service
    b) Build API Gateway using existing on premise public facing REST APIs as HTTPS endpoints integration type
    c) Use VPC Link to integrate on premise backend solutions through DirectConnect and private VPC

d) API Gateway cannot be integrated with on premise backend APIs which are not over public internet

67. Access control mechanisms for API Gateway; choose 2 from the following

   a) Usage Plans
   b) VPC Route Tables
   c) Server-side certificates
   d) Lambda authorizers
   e) Resource policies

68. Which of the following is not an action when enabling API caching for API gateway through console?

   a) Flush entire cache
   b) Refresh cache
   c) Encrypt cache data
   d) Cache capacity

69. To protect the backend systems, which of the following security measure is provided as default by the AWS in API Gateway?

   a) Security of backend systems fall under custom responsibility
   b) Protection from distributed denial-of-service (DDoS) attacks
   c) Default resource policy
   d) Default CORS configuration

70. Choose the correct statement for the given situation. You are receiving 8000 requests in one millisecond for your REST API. You created this API using AWS API Gateway with default throttle settings of 10000 requests per second with a burst of 5000 requests, and it is public facing.

   a) 5000 requests will succeed and throttles the rest 3000 in one-second period
   b) 5000 requests will succeed and rest 3000 will fail

c) All 8000 requests will fail as this is higher than the burst limit of 5000 requests

d) All 8000 requests will succeed as the default throttle limit is 8000 per second

71. The ABC company is planning to use ECS for docker applications, and also, they want to use third party monitoring tools for ECS instances. You are asked for recommendation, what would be your answer?

   a) ECS is a managed service. Customers cannot install 3rd party software
   b) Ask AWS to install trusted third party software
   c) Customers have control over ECS instances and monitoring can be setup like a normal EC2 instance
   d) Use CloudWatch for monitoring metrics

72. Choose 2 answers for this; you have launched an ECS cluster with 5 EC2 instances. Tasks are defined for this setup. But still, ECS is not receiving any status information from the container agent in each ECS instance. What could be the reason?

   a) You are running ECS on t2.micro instance which is not supported
   b) Interface VPC endpoint is not configured for ECS service
   c) Outbound rules of ECS instance's security group are not allowing traffic to ECS service endpoint
   d) Key-pair information is missing in ECS cluster
   e) IAM role used to run ECS instance does not have ecs:Poll action in its policy

73. For your ECS instance, you want to set ECS container agent configuration during ECS instance launch. How can this be done?

   a) Define configuration in service definition
   b) Define configuration is task definition
   c) Set configuration is user data parameter of ECS instance
   d) Set configuration in ECS metadata parameter during cluster creation

74. An organization, that actively uses AWS has noticed that some ECS clusters are running and they do not know by whom and when these clusters were created. You are asked find out the logs for this, how will you do this?

a) Check trusted advisor
b) Check CloudWatch metrics dashboard
c) Check CloudTrail logs
d) Check CloudWatch event logs

75. What parameters can be defined in service definition? (Choose 3)

a) IAM role that allows ECS to make calls to your load balancer on your behalf
b) Data volumes that should be used with the containers in the task
c) Environment variables that should be passed to the container when it starts
d) Task definition of the task definition to run in your service
e) Cluster on which to run your service

76. What parameters can be defined in task definition? (Choose 3)

a) Command that the container should run when it is started
b) VPC and subnets to launch containers in
c) How much CPU and memory to use with each container
d) EC2 instance types to be used as container instances
e) The docker images to use with the containers in your task

77. The valid launch type compatible with task definition based on where you want to launch your task. Choose from the following

a) Docker
b) AWS ECR
c) FARGATE
d) AWS VPC

78. Choose the statement that defines task definition

a) Template that defines actions for each IAM user on the ECS cluster
b) AWS managed service that launches ECS clusters

c) Template for a program that runs inside AWS ECS cluster

d) JSON template that describes containers which forms your application

79. Choose 3 features of AWS ECS

   a) Source image storage
   b) Cluster
   c) Container registry
   d) Tasks
   e) Task definition

80. Choose the correct statement in relation to ECS instances when accessing ECS service endpoint:

   a) AWS service endpoints are accessible internally across VPCs. You need to enable IAM access on the service which needs to be accessed
   b) Create a NAT gateway and attach it to VPC subnet's route table in which ECS instance is running
   c) ECS instances are launched with ECS-optimized AMI which contains an in-built mechanism to communicate with service endpoints through AWS network
   d) Create an interface VPC endpoint for ECS service and attach to VPC subnet's route table

81. Choose 2 event source from the following that are not supported by Lambda

   a) AWS OpsWorks
   b) AWS CodeCommit
   c) AWS CodePipeline
   d) AWS IoT
   e) AWS S3

82. Choose 2 options that are the responsibility of customer in AWS Lambda service

    a) Installing required libraries in underlying compute instances for Lambda execution
    b) Security patches
    c) Monitoring and logging
    d) Lambda function code
    e) Providing access to AWS resources which triggers Lambda function

83. Which of the following is not a potential use case for using AWS Lambda?

    a) A website with highly scaled backend layer which will persist data into RDS or DynamoDB
    b) Scheduled job to generate AWS resource usage reports based on certain tags
    c) Download S3 bucket objects of size varying between 500 MB-2 GB to a Lambda Ephemeral disk or temp location
    d) Periodically check log files for errors in CloudWatch or CloudTrail and send notifications through SNS

84. You configured Lambda function with SQS as event source. What is the maximum batch size that SQS supports for ReceiveMessage call?

    a) 100
    b) 10
    c) 40
    d) 20

85. Choose 3 CloudFront events that can trigger Lambda@edge function

    a) Origin response
    b) Origin request
    c) Viewer request
    d) Sender request
    e) CloudFront cache

86. Choose 3 poll based event sources for AWS Lambda function

    a) CodePipeline
    b) DynamoDB
    c) SQS
    d) Kinesis
    e) SNS

87. Choose 3 ARNs for Lambda function

    a) arn:aws:lambda:aws-region:acct-id:function:helloworld/1
    b) arn:aws:lambda:aws-region:acct-id:function:helloworld/PROD
    c) arn:aws:lambda:aws-region:acct-id:function:helloworld/$LATEST
    d) arn:aws:lambda:aws-region:acct-id:function:helloworld
    e) arn:aws:lambda:aws-region:acct-id:function:helloworld:$LATEST

88. Choose the valid Lambda configuration from the following

    a) 3072 MB memory and 300 seconds timeout
    b) 2112 MB memory and 10 seconds timeout
    c) 1376 MB memory and 120 seconds timeout
    d) 64 MB memory and 212 seconds timeout

89. Choose 2 AWS services where Lambda dead-letter queue pushes unprocessed events

    a) AWS X-Ray
    b) AWS CloudWatch
    c) AWS SNS
    d) AWS Kinesis
    e) AWS SQS

90. Choose 3 actions that are required by Lambda execution role to write the logs into AWS CloudWatch

   a) logs:GetLogEvents
   b) logs:DescribeLogStream
   c) logs:CreateLogGroup
   d) logs:CreateLogStream
   e) logs:PutLogEvents

91. For Lambda function, which one is not a CloudWatch metric?

   a) Invocations
   b) Duration
   c) Dead letter error
   d) Memory

92. For default retry behavior of AWS Lambda, which of the following is not true?

   a) With poll-based event sources that are not stream-based, if the invocation fails or times out, the message will be returned to the queue and will be available for invocation once the visibility timeout period expires
   b) With poll-based event sources, when a Lambda function invocation fails, Lambda attempts to process the erring batch of records until the time the data expires, which can be up to 7 days
   c) With asynchronous invocation, if Lambda is unable to fully process the event and if you don't specify a dead-letter queue, the event will be discarded
   d) With asynchronous invocation, the invoking application receives a 429 error and is responsible for retries

93. Your organization wants you to create a Lambda function in production mode and for auditing compliance, it is required that the production grade cost must not be modified when it is in execution. The modification first must go through a change process. To do so, you are going to publish version for PROD, you created an alias, you will use this

alias ARN to invoke the Lambda function. After all this, you are now told that the code should not run if the version is $LATEST. Choose 2 options to achieve the desired goal

   a) Use AWS_LAMBDA_FUNCTION_ALIAS environment variable
   b) Use AWS_LAMBDA_FUNCTION_VERSION environment variable
   c) Get invokedLambdaARN from event object and find out version from it
   d) getFunctionVersion from context object

94. To receive messages from an SQS queue and process the message body, you have setup SQS event trigger as Lambda function. After processing the message body, the function will insert one record in MySQL RDS instance. To connect the RDS instance, you need MySQL details such as homepage, username and password. How will you configure them?

   a) Store such configuration in S3 bucket and enable encryption on the bucket. Perform S3 getObject to get the configuration details
   b) Use properties file in AWS Lambda function for any such configuration. Properties files are encrypted by AWS is transit and at rest
   c) Use environment variable to pass configuration. Use encryption helpers to encrypt sensitive information by your own KMS key. Decrypt the variable using decryption helper code provided in the console
   d) Use environment variables to pass configuration. They are automatically encrypted by AWS default KMS keys and decrypted when used in Lambda function

95. You are required to create a Lambda function inside a VPC to communicate with RDS instance which is also inside the same VPC. You allocated 1 GB memory for the Lambda function. The expected number of concurrent requests during peak is 100. To run this Lambda function successfully, what should be the subnet range you should choose?

   a) /27
   b) /26
   c) /25
   d) /24

96. For development and testing, an organization has two different accounts as Dev and Test. They have a number of applications running on the Test account that require to trigger Lambda on Dev account. You are required to set a permission model to get this configuration working. What will you do?

    a) Add permission for Test account on Dev account's lambda function policy through AWS console
    b) Add permission for Test account on Dev account's lambda execution role policy through AWS CLI
    c) Add permission for Test account on Dev account's lambda execution role policy through AWS console
    d) Add permission for Test account on Dev account's lambda function policy through AWS CLI

97. Your team has many applications running on EC2 instances that need a common backend processing job. You created and published PROD version of the lambda function as version 1 to make sure that, if anyone changes the function, the change will not impact the PROD execution code. Assuming that, the requests would be sent to specific version, you shared the version qualified ARN to all the applications. After all this, because of frequent changes in requirements, you had to change the lambda code many times and keep publishing versions. This is a lot of overhead at the application level to update the Lambda function ARN each time you publish a new version. How can you overcome this situation?

    a) Do not use versioning in this case. Always use $LATEST version and share its ARN with applications. You can update the code of $LATEST version any number of times
    b) Delete the old published version 1 before publishing new version. So, when you publish, you will get the version ID as 1 lambda version ARN will remain unchanged
    c) Do not publish versions for every code change. Instead, update the published version
    d) Create an alias, point it to PROD version and share the ARN with apps. When new version is published, change the alias to point to it

98. To process the files that are uploaded to S3, you created a lambda function that started receiving requests and was working properly. Now, you have changed the code and updated the lambda function. What will happen to the requests now?

    a) Requests might be served by old or new version for a brief period of less than one minute
    b) When you have multiple versions of lambda function, you need to define in the code the version to be used.
    c) Requests will be served by old version until you set the new version as latest
    d) Requests will queue until the changes are fully propagated

99. An organization has AWS setup with DirectConnect. They have shifted many on premise backend applications to EC2 instances that have processes running based on triggers from other applications. These processes are developed using Java. Now they want you to migrate these processes to lambda to reduce the cost incurred on EC2 instances. What will you do?

    a) AWS lambda is not designed to run backend applications
    b) Trigger lambda from CloudWatch scheduled event and invoke CloudWatch API from your applications
    c) Replicate the Java code easily onto lambda function and use lambda invoke API with input passed as custom event
    d) Lambda cannot be invoked from custom application. They can only be triggered by AWS supported event sources

100. To perform daily health checks on your applications that are running on a fleet of 20 EC2 instances, you have planned to schedule a daily job with CloudWatch scheduled event with lambda function as trigger. To achieve this, EC2 instance's name tags has to be provided to identify the right resources. For this scenario, what is the correct way to pass the inputs?

    a) "Details" object of "Matched Event" can be configured while creating CloudWatch scheduled event
    b) You can set "Constant (JSON text)" option while selecting lambda as trigger for CloudWatch scheduled event

c) You can modify the "Matched Event" option while selecting lambda as trigger for CloudWatch scheduled events

d) Configure "Variables" option on CloudWatch scheduled event

101. Your company wants you to create a lambda function to read data from Kinesis stream of transactions. You created this function using context logger in the code to log the data to CloudWatch so that it can be monitored later. After the function started running along with Kinesis stream, you did not see any log entries for the new lambda function. What could be the reason?

a) Active tracing is not enabled on the lambda function

b) Lambda function execution logs can only be written to CloudTrail

c) Lambda execution role policy does not have access to create CloudWatch logs

d) Lambda function with Kinesis stream cannot write logs to CloudWatch

102. To launch an operation, your organization requires you to create a REST API. You are going to create this API using AWS API gateway with lambda as backend system and Oracle RDS instance as database. You have created API methods, lambda function code and launched the Oracle RDS instance in a private VPC which does not have an internet gateway. However, connection getting failed when you are trying to connect to RDS from your lambda function. Why? (Choose 2 reasons)

a) Lambda execution role does not have policy to access RDS instance

b) RDS instance is not configured as destination in lambda setup

c) Lambda function is running in same VPC as RDS, but RDS instance security group is not allowing connections from lambda subnet range

d) Lambda function is running in "no VPC" network mode

103. A team of data analysts need you. They need to perform big data analysis to transform data and store the results in S3. They were doing this with a lambda function. But, sometimes, the execution gets terminated abruptly after 5 minutes. They are asking you to enable notifications for such termination situations. How will you do this?

a) Configure Dead-letter queue (DLQ) and send notification to SNS topic

b) Configure SES for failures under configuration option in lambda function

c) Setup a timer, when it reaches 300, send a notification
d) Setup ERROR_NOTIFY environment variable with email addresses

104.   You are required to upload large files (1 GB – 3 GB) to S3 and calculate the hash checksum of the file to identify any potential corruption in downloads. This can be done by reading the entre file. Against these requirements, you created a lambda function with S3 notifications to trigger it. When you tested your function, the request is getting timed out. Why?

a) Lambda function and S3 bucket are in different regions
b) S3 bucket name is not setup in the environment variable
c) Lambda function is set to run in a private VPC without NAT gateway or VPC endpoint
d) Lambda function is configured with minimal memory (128 MB)

105.   Company PQRS, uploads compressed files to S3. These files are relatively large (100-200 MB). When upload completes, the total number of objects in the compressed files is added as the metadata of the file. They have hired you for a cost effective solution for this scenario. You recommended that they should use AWS lambda with S3 event notifications. For that, they are concerned about failures. S3 event notification is an asynchronous one-time trigger and lambda can fail due to operation timeouts, max memory limits, ma execution time limits etc. What could be the best retry approach?

a) Enable active tracing using AWS X-Ray to automatically retrigger failed events
b) All failures can be caught during exception inside lambda function
c) Configure DLQ with SQS, configure SQS to trigger lambda function again
d) All the failed events will be logged to CloudWatch; you can manually retrigger failed events

106.   An organization is planning to move its on premise infrastructure to the AWS cloud and is in need to migrate the virtual machines. You have been approached for recommendation, what would you suggest?

a) AWS EC2
b) AWS S3

c) AWS VM Import
d) AWS SQS

107. In your organization, the IT management wants you to build a web based application on AWS. The application should follow a serverless architecture to minimize the infrastructure cost. Choose 3 services that can be used for this requirement

   a) EC2
   b) DynamoDB
   c) Lambda
   d) API Gateway

108. Your company is planning to setup a content serving web application where users can access the content from all over the world. You are required to make sure that the users from any place in the world, can experience smooth and continuous performance of the web. Which of the following should definitely be part of this application?

   a) Amazon CloudFront
   b) Amazon CloudTrail
   c) Amazon SES
   d) Amazon S3

109. You work for an organization that want you to setup a hybrid connection between the on premises infrastructure and AWS VPC via AWS VPN managed connections. As an architect, which 2 from the following you will need for the connection to be established?

   a) Optical fiber cables
   b) An AWS DirectConnect device
   c) VPG
   d) A hardware compatible VPN device

110. As an AWS architect, you are asked to host an application using EC2 instances. The architecture should be fault tolerant and can be scaled on demand. Which 2 from the following will be included in your solution?

    a) AWS CloudWatch
    b) AWS ECS
    c) AWS ELB
    d) AWS Autoscaling

111. Your company wants you to connect an RDS instance to a web application. You have to make sure that the queries result should be delivered in a faster manner, also the performance of the database must be up to the mark. How will you achieve this?

    a) Amazon DynamoDB
    b) Amazon ElastiCache
    c) Amazon RDS for MySQL with multi-AZ
    d) MySQL installed on two EC2 instances in a single availability zone

112. Your main revenue generating application uses the table in the data store that is setup on AWS DynamoDB. Now you are expanding this application to 2 different other locations. To make sure that the data retrieval latency is the least from the new regions, which of the following you would choose?

    a) Place an ElastiCache in front of DynamoDB
    b) Enable global tables for DynamoDB
    c) Enable Multi-AZ for DynamoDB
    d) Place a cloud distribution in front of the database

113. You have setup EC2 instances in VPC for your application. Your organization is now worried that not all of the instances are in use. How AWS helps you in finding out underutilized resources? (Choose 2)

    a) CloudTrail
    b) SNS
    c) CloudWatch

d) AWS Trusted Advisor

114. An organization that has large SQL data sets is planning to move its applications on AWS cloud. The data sets are required to be hosted in a data store which should has disaster recovery features available. Which of the following you will choose for this?

a) Amazon SQS
b) Amazon Kinesis
c) Amazon RedShift
d) Amazon DynamoDB

115. As an architect in your company, you have setup EC2 instances in a VPC for your application. It is required to monitor all traffic to the instances. Which of the following features can be used to capture information for incoming and outgoing IP traffic from network interfaces in a VPC?

a) AWS VPC Flow Logs
b) AWS SQS
c) AWS EC2
d) AWS CloudWatch

116. Your company wants to stream the logs from their 100 servers on the AWS cloud for analysis. There will be programs running to analyze the stream of data for any sort of abnormal behavior. Which of the following services you would choose to stream the log data?

a) SES
b) Kinesis
c) SQS
d) CloudFront

117. Your organization is planning on a micro services based architecture which will include the deployment of various Docker containers. For this to get done, which service is ideal?

a) CodeCommit

b) Elastic Container Service

c) Simple Queue Service

d) DynamoDB

118. Your organization has decided to use API Gateway service to manage their APIs. Which of the following services are automatically integrated with the API Gateway to ensure better response?

a) AWS Lambda

b) AWS Volume gateway

c) CloudFront

d) CloudWatch

119. You have setup EC2 instances in a VPC. These instances are for your application. The security team wants to know the security mechanisms available to protect the instances in terms of incoming and outgoing IP traffic. What are the two layers of the security provided by AWS?

a) Route tables

b) DHCP options

c) Security groups

d) NACLs

120. Which of the following security features of the API Gateway can be used to make sure that the resources of the API can receive requests from a domain that is other than the API's domain?

a) API Access

b) API CORS

c) API Deployment

d) API Stages

121. You need at least eighth m4.large instances to serve traffic in your system. Your organization has this system in the us-east-1 region which has six availability zones. You

are asked to design this system in such a way that it can handle the death of a full availability zone. Cost saving is also needed. For all this, how are you going to distribute the servers? Assume that all the nodes are properly linked to an ELB, and you VPC account can utilize the region's AZs through f, inclusive.

a) 4 servers in each of AZs through c, inclusive
b) 2 servers in each of AZs through e, inclusive
c) 8 servers in each of AZs a and b
d) 3 servers in each of AZs through d, inclusive

122. You are asked to implement disaster recovery for an application that is currently running in the Singapore region. Meaning that, if the application goes down in Singapore, it has to be started in the Asia region. The subject app relies on pre-built AMIs, what DR strategy would you consider?

a) Modify the image permissions to share the AMI with another account, then set the default region to backup region
b) Modify the image permissions to share the AMI to the Asia region
c) Copy the AMI from Singapore to Asia region, modify the auto scaling groups in the backup region to use the new AMI ID in the backup region
d) Nothing, because all AMIs are available by default in every region

123. The organization that you work for has asked you to make them able to run analytics for all the combined log files from the ELB. Which combination of the services is used to collect log files and perform log file analysis in the AWS environment?

a) S3 to store ELB log files and EMR for processing these files in the analysis
b) S3 to store ELB log files and EC2 for processing these files in the analysis
c) EC2 for storing and processing the log files
d) DynamoDB to store the log files and EC2 for running custom log analysis scripts

124. How can you deploy a different application quickly to AWS, which are built using different programming languages and are different from each other?

a) Develop each app in a separate Docker container and deploy it using CloudFormation

b) Develop each app in a separate Docker container and deploy using Elastic BeanStalk

c) Create a lambda function deployment package consisting of code and dependencies

d) Develop each app in one Docker container and deploy using Elastic BeanStalk

125. Your organization requires to keep the application log files for ten years. The most recent log files are needed regularly for troubleshooting. It is required to keep the logging system cost-effective and can be given large volumes of log data. How can you achieve this?

a) Store logs on EBS, and use EBS snapshots to archive them

b) Store logs in S3, use lifecycle policies to archive Amazon Glacier

c) Store logs in Amazon Glacier

d) Store logs in Amazon CloudWatch logs

126. You are building environment for an application on AWS. To make the auditing environment easy and security compliant, which service or feature you need to enable?

a) Multi-factor authentication

b) Encrypted data storage

c) SSL logging

d) CloudTrail for security logs

127. You need to design an application that should have; EC2 as a web server, session data to be written on DynamoDB, and log files to be written on MS SQL server. How are you going to make sure that the data is written to a DynamoDB table?

a) Create an IAM role that allows write access to the DynamoDB table

b) Create an IAM role that allows read access to the DynamoDB table

c) Add an IAM user that allows write access to the DynamoDB table

d) Add an IAM user to a running EC2 instance

128. As a solutions architect, you proposed an idea of moving your organization's development, test, and production applications on EC2 instances. The seniors are

worried about how the access control would be given to related IT admins. What would you suggest for this concern?

a) Add each environment to a separate auto scaling group
b) Add Metadata to the underlying instances to mark each environment
c) Add Userdata to the underlying instances to mark each environment
d) Add tags to the instances marking each environment then segregate access using IAM policies

129. Your company requires a data storage layer for storage of JSON documents. Other requirements are the availability of indexes and auto-scaling. Which of the following would you choose to meet the requirements?

a) AWS Glacier
b) AWS S3
c) AWS EBS volumes
d) AWS DynamoDB

130. Your organization needs a data processing system on AWS. Which of the following would you choose to build this system?

a) AWS ECR
b) AWS ECS
c) AWS EMR
d) AWS DynamoDB

131. You are assigned with a task of setting up a public website with database and application server running in a VPC. The database should be able to connect to the internet for patch upgrades. There should be no incoming requests to the database from the internet. Which of the following solutions would best satisfy all these requirements?

a) Set up the public website on a public subnet and set up the database in a private subnet which connects to the internet via a NAT instance
b) Set up the database in a local data center and use the private gateway to connect the application to the database

c) Set up the database in a public subnet with a security group which only allows inbound traffic

d) Set up the database in a private subnet with a security group which only allows outbound traffic

132.   For your company, you developed a mobile app with DynamoDB as the backend and JavaScript as the frontend. You have notices spikes in the app especially in the DynamoDB area, which of the following provides scalable and the most cost-effective architecture for this application?

a) Launch DynamoDB with multi-AZ configuration with a global index to balance writes

b) Create a service that pulls SQS messages and writes these to DynamoDB to handle sudden spikes in DynamoDB

c) Increase write capacity of DynamoDB to meet the peak loads

d) Auto scale DynamoDB to meet the requirements

133. For warehousing, your organization has petabyte-scale data in a RedShift cluster which can be easily reproduced from additional data that is stored in S3. You are asked to find a way of reducing the overall cost of running this cluster. From the given options, which one would best meet the needs of the running cluster while reducing overall ownership of the cluster?

a) Implement daily backups, but do not enable multi-region copy to save the cost of data transfer

b) Disable automated and manual snapshots on the cluster

c) Enable automated snapshots but set the retention period to a lower number to reduce storage cost

d) Instead of implementing automatic daily backups, write a CLI script that creates manual snapshots every few days. Copy the manual snapshots to a secondary AWS region for DR situations

134.   The company that you work for requires a large-scale confidential web server which can store documentation on S3. It is necessary that, by using CloudFront, it should not

be publicly accessible from S3 directly. Which of the following satisfies the mentioned requirements?

   a) Create an S3 bucket policy that lists the CloudFront distribution ID as the principal and the target bucket ID as ARN
   b) Create individual policies for each bucket in which the documents are stored, and grant access only to CloudFront
   c) Create and origin access identity (OAI) for CloudFront and grant access to the objects in your S3 bucket to that OAI
   d) Create an IAM user for CloudFront and grant access to the objects in your S3 bucket for that IAM user

135.   While performing a load test on your application's MySQL DB instance, you noticed that when CPU utilization reaches 100%, the application becomes unresponsive. Considering that your application is read-heavy, what methods will help in scaling your data-tier to meet the needs of your application? (Choose 3)

   a) Enable multi-AZ for your DB instance
   b) Shard your data set among multiple Amazon RDS DB instances
   c) Use EalstiCache in front of your RDS instance to cache common queries
   d) Use SQS queue to throttle data going to RDS instance
   e) Add your RDS instance to an auto scaling group and configure CloudWatch metric based on CPU utilization
   f) Add DB read replicas, and have your application direct read queries to them

136.   You want to use ECS and utilize the set of Docker images that you have for building containers. Which of the following can be used to store these Docker images?

   a) Use the ECR service to store the Docker images
   b) Use EC2 instances with EBS volumes to store Docker images
   c) Use AWS RDS to store Docker images
   d) Use DynamoDB to store Docker images

137.   You are asked if you can deploy an existing Java application to AWS with auto scaling for the underlying environment. Which of the following would you choose to do the task in the quickest way possible?

    a) Use AMIs to build EC2 instances for deployment
    b) Use EC2 with auto scaling for the environment
    c) Use the Elastic BeanStalk service to provision the environment
    d) Deploy to an S3 bucket and enable website hosting

138.   To monitor the number of bags handled at an airport, the management has placed IoT sensors. A default-set Kinesis stream receives the data and then on every alternate day, this data is sent to S3 for processing. They have noticed that S3 is not receiving all of the data that is sent to the Kinesis stream. What do you think could be the reason?

    a) Kinesis streams are not meant to handle IoT related data
    b) Data records are only accessible for a default time of 24 hours
    c) S3 can only store data for a day
    d) The sensors probably stopped working on some days. Hence data is not sent to the stream

139.   You need to host a database on EC2, and an EBS volume is required to support a high rate of IOPS because you are expecting a large number of read and write requests. Which Amazon EBS volume type can meet the requirements of this database?

    a) EBS Cold HDD
    b) EBS General Purpose SSD
    c) EBS Throughput Optimized HDD
    d) EBS Provisioned IOPS SSD

140.   Which of the following would be optimal to upload a million files to S3?

    a) Use a sequential ID for the suffix
    b) Use a date for the suffix
    c) Use a hexadecimal hash for the prefix
    d) Use a date for the prefix

141. A group of data analysts reached you for a recommendation; they need a columnar structured database to perform complex analytic queries against petabytes of data. Which AWS service would you recommend?

    a) DynamoDB
    b) ElastiCache
    c) Amazon RDS
    d) Amazon RedShift

142. You are assigned with a task of building a highly available and fault-tolerant application architecture. This architecture has to be loosely coupled. You have decided to use EC2, the classic load balancer, auto-scaling, and Route 53. Which of the following services should you also involve in this architecture?

    a) AWS Config
    b) AWS API Gateway
    c) AWS SQS
    d) AWS SNS

143. You have instances running in a private subnet, and the management has asked you to make sure that these instances can access the internet. Your solution should be highly available and should cause less maintenance overhead. What would you do to meet this requirement?

    a) Use NAT Gateway in the public subnet
    b) Use NAT Gateway in the private subnet
    c) Host the NAT instance in the public subnet
    d) Host the NAT instance in the private subnet

144. You, a solutions architect in an organization, have been tasked with architecting an application that consists of EC2, the classic load balancer, auto-scaling, and Route 53. It is a must to make this architecture in a way that Blue-Green deployments are possible. What could be the ideal routing policy to use in Route 53 to fulfil the requirements?

a) Weighted
b) Latency
c) Multi-answer
d) Simple

145. Your organization uses different accounts for different departments. You are asked to connect two VPCs that are running in development and production accounts. How will you achieve this?

a) Use VPC peering
b) Use consolidated billing for both accounts
c) Use the VPC route tables to map both the VPCs
d) Use security groups to map both VPCs

146. A company has an application that requires an EC2 instance to perform log processing with 500 MiB/s of data throughput. They are planning to deploy it to the AWS cloud. They have approached you for storage recommendation, what would you suggest?

a) EBS Cold Storage
b) EBS Throughput Optimized
c) EBS SSD
d) EBS IOPS

147. One of your friends wants you to deploy his code functions in the AWS cloud, but he doesn't want to manage the infrastructure. Which of the following services can fulfil his desire?

a) DynamoDB
b) Lambda
c) API Gateway
d) EC2

148. You are requested to create a web application for a media company. Using this app, users will upload the pictures that they have created to be published on the web.

Considering requirements, you know that this application must be able to call the S3 API, without it, this can't function. Where should you store API credentials while maintaining the maximum level of security?

a) Pass API credentials to the instance using instance user data
b) Save your API credentials in a public GitHub repository
c) Don't save your API credentials, instead, create an IAM role and assign this role to an EC2 instance when you first create it
d) Save the API credentials to your PHP files

149. Users subscribe to your web application by using their email IDs. You want to enable them to receive messages that are published by the service. Which of the following service can probably be included in this architecture?

a) AWS Glacier
b) AWS S3
c) AWS Config
d) AWS SNS

150. Your company wants you to keep a check on the active EBS volumes, active snapshots, and Elastic IP addresses that your organization use. Also, ensure that you don't go beyond the service limit. Which service will be helpful in this regard?

a) SNS
b) Trusted Advisor
c) EC2
d) CloudWatch

151. You work in an organization as a solutions architect; they want you to manage a RedShift cluster and monitor its performance to make sure that it is working efficiently as possible. What services would you use for fulfilling this requirement?

a) Trusted Advisor
b) CloudWatch
c) VPC Flow logs

d) CloudTrail

152. A person who uses S3 for storage wants you to make sure that his data is encrypted. But, he doesn't want to manage the encryption keys. You know a lot, can you tell him the encryption mechanism that could help him in this case?

   a) SSE-SSL
   b) SSE-KMS
   c) SSE-C
   d) SSE-S3

153. You have set up an S3 bucket for your company which is accessed quite frequently. The management wants you to implement something that could reduce the cost of accessing it. What step would you take to do this?

   a) Place the S3 bucket behind an API Gateway
   b) Enable encryption on the S3 bucket
   c) Enable versioning on the S3 bucket
   d) Place the S3 bucket behind a CloudFront distribution

154. Your organization is in Seoul, and your EC2 instance is in the same region, i.e., the Asia Pacific. A preconfigured software is running on this instance, and you are requested to make DR solution if the instance in the region fails. What could be the best solution for this?

   a) Create an AMI of the EC2 instance and copy it to another region
   b) Store the EC2 data on S3. If the instance fails, bring up a new instance and restore the data from S3
   c) Backup the EBS data volume. If the instance fails, bring up a new instance and attach the volume
   d) Create a duplicate instance in another AZ and keep its state as shutdown. If the instance fails, start the duplicate instance

155.   You have been tasked to create a cost-effective solution. The scenario is, users will upload the videos, and after a defined period (a month), these videos can be deleted. What will you do?

    a) Store the videos using stored volumes. Create a script to delete the videos after a month
    b) Store the videos in Amazon Glacier and use lifecycle policies
    c) Use transition rule in S3 to move the files to Glacier and use expiration rule to delete it after 30 days
    d) Use EBS volumes to store the videos, create a script to delete the videos after a month

156.   The company that you work for is required to have an ability of data archival. They want this ability in a cost-efficient way, what would you do?

    a) S3 Standard
    b) EFS
    c) S3 Standard-IA
    d) Glacier

157.   A group of Ph.D. students is in need of a fully managed NoSQL database on the cloud. They asked you for a highly available and backup enabled database solution. Which Amazon database would you suggest?

    a) Aurora
    b) DynamoDB
    c) MS SQL
    d) MySQL

158.   You are hosting a MySQL database for your company using AWS RDS service. To offload the reads, you created a read replica and made the reports flee to the read replica database. However, you are noticing that the reports show old data. Why do you think it is happening?

    a) Multi-AZ feature is not enabled

b) The replication is lagging
c) Backup of original database is not set properly
d) The read replica has not been created properly

159. An idea of building a 2 tier architecture is floating in your organization. This architecture will be containing a web server and a database server that is hosted on EC2 instances. Heavy read/write operations are expected on the database server while the web server will have a standard load of work. You, as a solutions architect, which EBS volumes would you choose for optimum performance? Choose 2; one for the web server and the other for the database.

a) Provisioned IOPS for the database server
b) General Purpose SSD for the database server
c) Provisioned IOPS for the web server
d) General Purpose SSD for the web server

160. You have hosted your company's web server on an EC2 instance. A larger part of the CPU is being consumed by the number of requests, resulting in degraded performance of the application. What would you do to diminish the problem to provide a better response time?

a) Place a CloudFront distribution in front of the EC2 instance
b) Place the EC2 instance in an auto-scaling group
c) Place the EC2 instance behind an application load balancer
d) Place the EC2 instance behind a classic load balancer

161. To make the best use of the serverless aspects of the AWS cloud, you have decided to use SQS and Lambda services. Each call to Lambda function will add a message in the SQS queue. To send the messages, which of the following you must do?

a) An IAM group with the required permissions
b) The code for lambda must be written in C#
c) An IAM role with required permissions
d) The queue must be FIFO queue

162.   You have set the data layer for your organization in S3. There are a lot of requests that include read/write and updates to the objects in the S3 bucket. A complaint has arisen; users are saying that the updates to an object are not reflected. What could be the reason for this?

    a) Metadata for the S3 bucket is not correctly configured
    b) Encryption is enabled for the bucket which causes a delay in updates
    c) Updates are being made to the same key for the object
    d) Versioning is not enabled, so the newer versions do not reflect the right data

163.   An organization is planning to move to the cloud; they want to use their existing chef recipes for configuration management of their infrastructure. Which AWS service do you think is ideal for them?

    a) AWS Inspector
    b) AWS OpsWorks
    c) AWS Elastic BeanStalk
    d) AWS Elastic Load Balancer

164.   Your company is planning to host a web application that contains a web server and a database server. You work for this company as a solutions architect, you have planned to host these servers on different EC2 instances in different subnets inside a VPC. Which of the following would you use to ensure that the database server only allows traffic from the web server?

    a) Use IAM roles
    b) Use NACLs
    c) Use VPC Flow logs
    d) Use security groups

165.   For the AWS account that is in use of your organization, you have enabled CloudTrail logs. The IT security department also wants these logs to be encrypted. How will you fulfil their requirement?

    a) Enable server-side encryption for the destination S3 bucket

b) Enable server-side encryption for the trail

c) There is no need to do anything as logs are automatically encrypted

d) Enable SSL certificates for the CloudTrail logs

166. You have a web application that contains two servers, i.e., web and database servers. These servers are hosted on separate EC2 instances. Heavy read requests on the database are degrading the performance of your application. What can you do to improve the performance of your application?

a) Place a CloudFront distribution in front of the database

b) Place another web server in the architecture to take the load

c) Put an ElastiCache in front of the database

d) Enable multi-AZ for the database

167. The IT supervisor in your organization is fed up with the users that accidentally delete objects in an S3 bucket. Can you solve his problem? Is there any way to prevent accidental deletion? (Choose 2)

a) Enable IAM roles on the S3 bucket

b) Enable versioning on the S3 bucket

c) Enable MFA to delete on the S3 bucket

d) Enable encryption for the S3 bucket

168. Your organization has planned and wanted you to move their PostgreSQL database to the AWS cloud. Replicas of the database and automated backup are the key requirements. Which database service would ideally fit this scenario?

a) RedShift

b) DynamoDB

c) PostgreSQL

d) Aurora

169. A friend of yours works for an organization as a solutions architect; he is designing a solution to store and archive corporate documents, the data has to be retrieved within 3-5 hours as directed by the management. He has decided to use Amazon Glacier for

this. Now, he wants your suggestion about the features of Amazon Glacier that can help him in meeting the requirements while ensuring the cost-effectiveness. What would you suggest?

a) Standard retrieval
b) Bulk retrieval
c) Expedited retrieval
d) Vault lock

170. For document storage, users within your organization need a place. It is required that each user must have his/her own location for placing the objects and should not be able to see other user's documents. Document retrieval should be an easy process. Which AWS service do you think is ideal for this?

a) RDS MySQL
b) RedShift
c) Glacier
d) S3

171. You created a set of lambda functions and embedded business logics in them. You want to configure these functions in a way that the users can call these via HTTPS requests. How can this be achieved?

a) Use S3 websites to make calls to the lambda function
b) Add EC2 instances with an API server installed. Integrate the server with a lambda function
c) Enable HTTP access on the lambda functions
d) Use the API gateway and provide integration with lambda functions

172. You are using an S3 bucket as the data layer for your company's application. When monitoring the bucket, it has been noticed that there are 400 GET requests per second. The IT operations team receives requests of users who get HTTP 500 or 503 errors while accessing the application. What would you do to resolve these errors? (Choose 2)

a) Enable versioning for an S3 bucket

b) Add an ELB in front of the S3 bucket

c) Add randomness to the key names

d) Add a CloudFront distribution in front of the bucket

173. You have EBS backed EC2 instances for your organization. It is clearly stated in the organization's IT policy that it is must back up the data efficiently. You, as a solutions architect are responsible for a backup policy. What do you think is the most adaptable way to back up the EBS volumes?

a) Mirror data across two volumes

b) Write a script to copy data to an EC2 instance store

c) Enable EBS volume encryption

d) Take regular EBS snapshots

174. The organization that you work for have RedShift cluster with reserved instances because it has been running for a long duration of a couple of years. Automated and manual snapshots are enabled. These days, the cost being incurred by the cluster in under consideration. You, as a solutions architect, what measures would you make to minimize the cost?

a) Use instance store volumes to store the cluster data

b) Use spot instances instead of reserved instances

c) Set the retention period of the automated snapshots to 35 days

d) Delete the manual snapshots

175. Provide your company with an efficient way to store the backed up data on AWS that has been backed up from an on-premises hosted server.

a) Use Amazon Glacier

b) Use storage gateway stored volumes

c) Create EBS snapshots and store the data

d) Create EBS volumes and store the data

176. Your company has a VPC and a subnet with an instance in it. The instance has a public IP. When you attached an internet gateway (IGW) to the VPC, you see that the

instance still couldn't be reached from the internet. What changes should be made to the below-given route table?

Destination	Target	Status	Propagated
10.0.0.0/16	Local	Active	No

Please select:

    a) Add this entry to route table: 0.0.0.0/16 -> internet gateway
    b) Add this entry to route table: 10.0.0.0/16 -> internet gateway
    c) Modify the route table: 10.0.0.0/16 -> internet gateway
    d) Add this entry to route table: 0.0.0.0/0 -> internet gateway

177. PimPom company is planning to host their web application on an EC2 instance. It is expected that the users will increase in the coming months, so it is necessary to add elasticity to your system. What steps would you take to add elasticity to your setup? (Choose 2)

    a) Setup DynamoDB behind your EC2 instance
    b) Setup an ElastiCache in front of the EC2 instance
    c) Set up your app on more EC2 instances and set them behind an ELB
    d) Set up your app on more EC2 instances and use Route 53 to route requests accordingly

178. A solutions architect is assigned with a task of deploying Docker containers to the cloud. Those who hired him for this, also want a highly scalable service that can help in managing the coordination of these containers. What would be optimal for such a requirement?

    a) Use lambda functions to embed the logic for container coordination
    b) Use SQS to orchestrate the messages between Docker containers
    c) Install a custom tool for orchestration
    d) Use ECS service for Kubernetes

179.   Spin up the instances is an often occurring demand in your company. You have an auto-scaling group for this purpose. As an architect, what can you do to make sure that your instances are pre-installed with software when they are launched?
    a) IT operations team should install the software as an instance launches
    b) Add the software installation to the configuration of the auto-scaling group
    c) Add the scripts for the installation in the user data section
    d) Create a golden image and then create a launch configuration

180.   You are running a set of IIS servers on EC2 instances for your organization. The log files of these servers are needed to be collected and processed. Which AWS service would you choose for this requirement?

    a) DynamoDB to store the logs and EC2 for running custom log analysis scripts
    b) EC2 for storing and processing the logs
    c) S3 for storing the log files and EMR for processing the log files
    d) S3 for storing the log files and EC2 for processing the log files

181.   An organization named Chingchi has launched EC2 instances for non-production workloads. These instances are also used for non-priority batch loads. The given loads of work, as you know, can be interrupted at any time. For this scenario, which pricing model of the EC2 is the best?

    a) Regular instances
    b) Spot instances
    c) On-demand instances
    d) Reserved instances

182.   The management of your organization wants you to create a DR strategy for minimizing the cost of the resources in AWS. They want the ability of spinning up the architecture in another region. How will you do this while keeping the cost minimum?

    a) Use Elastic BeanStalk to create a copy of your infrastructure in another region if a disaster situation occurs in your primary region.
    b) Use CloudFormation to spin up resources in another region if a disaster occurs in the primary region

c) Create a pilot light infrastructure in another region

d) Create a duplicate of the entire infrastructure in another region

183. For high availability solutions, which AWS services do you think can be implemented in multiple AZs? (Choose 2)

a) Amazon S3
b) Amazon DynamoDB
c) EC2
d) ELB

184. You are asked to build a stateless application with auto-scaled web servers. What do you think would be the ideal storage mechanism for storing session data?

a) S3
b) EBS Volumes
c) DynamoDB
d) RedShift

185. To ensure multi-region availability of objects in an S3 bucket, what do you think is the easiest way?

a) Enable versioning which will copy the objects to the destination region
b) Enable cross-region replication for the bucket
c) Write a script to copy the objects to another bucket in the destination region
d) Create an S3 snapshot in the destination region

186. An organization used incident based application hosted on EC2 instances which are placed after the auto scaling group. The organization is facing low performance of the application in the morning at 8:30 AM although the use of autoscaling group give surety that some instances are in place to support the application. In what way we optimized the performance of the application at 8:30 AM.

a) Change cooldown timer for the existing auto scaling group
b) Create another Dynamic scaling policy to ensure that scaling happens at 8:30 AM
c) Add a scheduled scaling policy at 7:30 AM

d) Add another auto scaling group to support the current one

187. Which is most quick and cost-effective way to host a static website in AWS? (choose any 2)
a) Upload code to the web server on the EC2 instance
b) Create an EC2 instance and install a web server
c) Upload static content to an S3 bucket
d) Enable website hosting for an S3 bucket

188. An organization required that it's domain name points to an existing CloudFront distribution, and they are planning to use Route53 as DNS provider. Which solution meets the need?
a) Create a host record which points to the CloudFront distribution
b) Create non-alias record which points to the CloudFront distribution
c) Create a CNAME record which points to the CloudFront distribution
d) Create an Alias record which points to the CloudFront distribution

189. A set of applications use Docker containers. How to shift these Docker containers in a separate environment in AWS?
a) Create EBS optimized EC2 instances, install Docker and then upload the containers
b) Create EC2 instances, install Docker and then upload the containers
c) Create EC2 container registries, install Docker and then upload the containers
d) Create an Elastic Beanstalk environment with necessary Docker containers

190. A photo is shared on the website, and with the use of S3 this photo is served to the visitors of the website, but other websites are also linking to the photo of your site and make a loss in business. Which solution do you choose to reduce this effect?
a) Use CloudFront distributions for static content
b) Store photos on an EBS volume of the web server
c) Remove public read access and use signed URLs with expiry dates
d) Block the IPs of that website in the security group

191. How you manage the infrastructure which has No-SQL database hosted on AWS cloud?
a) AWS DynamoDB
b) AWS RDS

c) AWS ElatiCache
d) AWS Redshift

192. Which AWS service supports the development of a new application which has a microservices architecture? (choose 2)
a) AWS Config
b) AWS Lambda
c) AWS API gateway
d) AWS Cloud trail

193. Which is a most effective way to detect errors in running script on AWS Lambda service?
a) Use AWS Config service to monitor errors
b) Use AWS trusted advisor service to monitor errors
c) Use AWS Cloudwatch metrics and logs to watch errors
d) Use AWS Cloutrail service to monitor errors

194. An organization stored critical data in Amazon S3 and also need that data will be available in the different geographical location. Which solution meets the above requirements?
a) Copy data to an EBS volume in another region
b) Copy snapshot of S3 bucket in another region
c) Enable cross-region replication for an S3 bucket
d) Apply Multi-AZ for an underlying S3 bucket

195. The client wants to store data in AWS, and after one year he wants to delete that data but before one year that data is frequent access by the client. Which architect is best for given requirements?

a) Store the file in Amazon S3 and create lifecycle policy to remove the file after one year
b) Store the file in Amazon Glacier and create a lifecycle policy to remove the file after one year
c) Store the file in Amazon snowball and create lifecycle policy to remove the file after one year
d) Store the file in Amazon storage gateway and create lifecycle policy to remove the file after one year

196.   Which AWS service is best to monitor database metrics hosted on AWS and send a notification? (choose 2)

a) Amazon Cloudwatch
b) Amazon Simple email service
c) Amazon Route53
d) Amazon Simple notification service

197.   If you have data in EBS volumes and they are frequently accessed in 1 month, and after that, you need to move these data to infrequent access storage. Which storage is cost-effective storage of EBS volume type to meet the requirements?

a) EBS Cold HDD
b) EBS General purpose SSD
c) EBS Provisioned IOPS SSD
d) EBS Throughput Optimized HDD

198.   An organization wants to run an application with two EC2 instances in which one is for the database server, and the other is for a web application. Which solution helps to make the high availability of the database layer?

a) Enable Multi-AZ for database
b) Have another EC2 instance in same availability zone without replication configuration
c) Have another EC2 instance in another availability zone with replication configuration
d) Have another EC2 instance in same availability zone with replication configuration

199.   An organization has an application in which they need to add port 443 to a security group to make application working properly. How much time taken by an application to work properly after adding a port?

a) It takes an hour to propagate the rules
b) It takes 60 seconds for rules to apply to all AZ within the region
c) It works properly after rebooting EC2 instances belong to that security group

d) Changes applied to security group and application should be able to respond to 443 requests.

200. An organization has a setup of VPC with a subnet and internet gateway. They need to connect EC2 instance with internet although EC2 instance is set up with a public IP, and they are the wrong security group, but still, they are unable to connect to the internet. Which solution help to overcome this issue?

a) Ensure the right route entry in the route table
b) Set an Elastic IP address to EC2 instance
c) Check logs may be there is an issue in EC2 instance
d) Sat a secondary private IP address to EC2 instance

201. An organization is planning to deploy a critical application to AWS whose controls set meet PCI compliance. They also need to detect any malicious activity by monitoring logs of the web application. Which service meets the above requirement?

a) AWS OpsWork
b) Amazon CloudWatch Logs
c) Amazon AWS Config
d) Amazon CloudTrail

202. How you encrypt your critical data when you host an AWS RDS instance?

a) Enable encryption of the critical EBS volumes
b) Ensure that right instance class is chosen for critical data
c) Choose only General Purpose SSD because it will support encryption of data
d) Encrypt database during the creation

203. A company created AWS Lambda function to write data to the DynamoDB table. How they interact Lambda function with DynamoDB table?

a) Ensure the Access keys are embedded in AWS Lambda Function
b) Ensure IAM user password is embedded in AWS Lambda function
c) Ensure IAM role is attached to the Lambda function which has required DynamoDB privileges
d) Ensure IAM user is attached to the Lambda function which has required DynamoDB privileges

204.   An organization needs to run 150 GB relational database on EC2 instance. Which is the most cost-effective storage type used when an application frequently used for high read and writes operations.

a) Amazon EFS
b) Amazon EBS provisioned IOPS SSD
c) Amazon EBS Cold HDD
d) Amazon EBS general purpose HDD

205.   A company has an infrastructure on AWS in which private subnet contains database server, and public subnet contains NAT instance. Through NAT instance, instances in private subnet communicate with the internet. Now NAT instance become a barrier in architecture, how you overcome this problem?

a) Use VPC connection for better bandwidth
b) Consider changing the instance type for the underlying NAT instance
c) Use another internet gateway for better bandwidth
d) Use NAT gateway instead of NAT instance

206.   A video transcoding company runs an application of video transcoding on AWS EC2. Which video need to be transcoded an instance polls the queue and perform transcoding. Consider that process is interrupted and another instance transcodes video based on a queue system. Due to this a massive amount backlog of videos need to be transcoded, and they consider to add a new instance to reduce this backlog, and these instances will only be required until the backlog is reduced. Which Amazon EC2 instance type is best for this purpose?

a) On-demand instances
b) Reserved instances
c) Spot Instances
d) Dedicated Instances

207.   University hosts their architecture in Europe region and wants to duplicate this architecture in the Asia region and also want to expand the application in a new region

hosted in this architecture. Which solution is best to choose to ensure that the students from all over the world will experience the same from the setup?

a) Create a geolocation Route53 policy to route the policy based on locations
b) Create classic load balancer setup to route traffic to both locations
c) Create a weighted route53 policy to route the policy based in weightage for each location
d) Create an application elastic load balancer setup to route traffic for both locations

208. An organization host instance in the AWS public cloud. VPC and subnet to host instance are created with default network ACL. An administrator wants to provide secure access to the underlying instance. How they achieve that?

a) Ensure that the security group allows outbound SSH traffic from the administrator's workstation
b) Ensure that the Network ACL allow inbound SSH traffic from the administrator's workstation
c) Ensure that the security group allows inbound SSH traffic from the administrator's workstation
d) Ensure that the Network ACL allow outbound SSH traffic from the administrator's workstation

209. Which block-level storage device is used to store data on EC2 instances on AWS cloud?

a) Amazon EFS
b) Amazon EBS volumes
c) Amazon S3
d) Amazon Glacier

210. An organization create VPC from scratch and launch EC2 instances in the subnet. How are these instances accessible from the internet?

a) Attach a NAT gateway to VPC and add a route for 0.0.0.0/32 to the route table
b) Attach an internet gateway to VPC and add a route for 0.0.0.0/32 to the route table
c) Attach an internet gateway to VPC and add a route for 0.0.0.0/0 to the route table

d) Attach a NAT gateway to VPC and add a route for 0.0.0.0/0 to the route table

211. When your S3 bucket receives over 100 PUT requests per second then how you optimize the performance of your S3 bucket?

    a) Add random prefix to the key name
    b) Use a predictable naming scheme, such as sequential numbers or date-time sequences in the key name
    c) Use multipart upload
    d) Amazon S3 will automatically manage performance at this scale

212. An organization wants to host their application and web servers through the use of EC2 instances. In the space of automation, they want that instances download the latest version of web and application server when they are launched. Which solution fulfills the above requirements?

    a) Use auto scaling groups to install web and application servers when the instance launched
    b) Organization create scripts which can be added to the user data section when the instance is launched
    c) Use EC2 config to install the web and application server when the instances are launched
    d) The organization creates scripts which can be added to the Metadata section when instances are launched.

213. An institute wants VPC network topology which has internet facing and internal facing application, and both are accessible over VPN only, and both application also has the capability of at least 4 AZs for high availability. How many subnets need to be created in VPC to fulfill these requirements?

    a) 8
    b) 6
    c) 3
    d) 2

214.   An educational website is facing a high amount of traffic during exam season. How to configure DNS failover to a static website in case of load failure?

a) Add more servers in case it fails
b) Supplicate exact application architecture to another region and configure DNS Weight-based routing
c) Enable failover to an on-premises data center to an application hosted there
d) Use Route53 with failover option to a static S3 website bucket or CloudFront distribution

215.   An organization has two web servers instances assigned to ELB. Both the instances and ELB are not reachable via URL to ELB serving the web app data from EC2 instances. How the instances are serving web app data to the public internet?

a) Use Amazon ELB to serve requests to your instances located in internal subnet
b) Attach an Internet Gateway to VPC and route is to the subnet
c) Add an Elastic IP address to the instance
d) None of the above

216.   If you want to control access to S3 buckets, then how you can do that?

a) Use IAM user roles
b) Use bucket policies
c) Use IAM access keys
d) Use secure token service

217.   The client wants to work with a container with the help of AWS ECS service, and they need less administrative work during the launch of the container. Which solution meets the above requirement?

a) Use ELB launch type in AWS ECS
b) Use Auto-scaling launch type in AWS ECS
c) Use Fargate launch type in AWS ECS
d) Use EC2 launch type in AWS ECS

218. An organization has planning and deployment based instances running on your VPC, and both instances depend on different work. What is the secure way to ensure that people responsible for one instance do not have access to other instance?

   a) Launch the test and planning instances in different AZ and use Multi-Factor Authentication
   b) Define the tags on the test and planning servers and add a condition to IAM policy with allows access to specific tags
   c) Launch the test and planning instances in separate VPCs and use VPC peering
   d) Create IAM policy with the condition that allows access to only those instances which are used for planning or deployment

219. An organization hosted database in AWS and because of the huge amount of write operation database can't handle the load. Which solution gives surety that there is no loss in write operation under any scenario?

   a) Use SNS to send notification on missed database writes and then add them manually at a later stage
   b) Consider using ElastiCache instead of AWS RDS
   c) Consider using DynamoDB instead of AWS RDS
   d) Use SQS Queues to Queue the database writes

220. An institute store its student records in AWS S3 and they are worried if that records ever be deleted. How they make these record protected in S3?

   a) Create a snapshot of the S3 bucket
   b) Enable Versioning for an S3 bucket
   c) Enable IAM policy which does not allow deletion of any document from the bucket
   d) Copy bucket data to an EBS volume as a backup

221. An organization required extra storage infrastructure to AWS cloud and needed that storage available for on-premises application server as iSCSI devices. Which solution meets the above requirements?

   a) Use EFS file service and mount the different file system to on-premises servers
   b) Create glacier vault. Use glacier connector and mount it as an iSCSI device

c) Use AWS storage gateway-cached volumes service
d) Create an S3 bucket. Use S3 connector and mount it as an iSCSI device

222.   A company wants to access some critical data stored in S3 through instances which are in private subnet, but due to its privacy, you need to ensure that critical data do not traverse over the internet. Which solution fulfills the above requirement?

a) Move instance in public subnet
b) Consider using VPC endpoint
c) Consider using an EC2 endpoint
d) Create a VPN connection and access S3 resources from EC2 instance

223.   Which AWS service is helpful to create standard templates for infrastructure and then it will further used in case of disaster recovery to provide resources in another region?

a) AWS CloudFormation
b) AWS Elastic Beanstalk
c) AWS CloudFront
d) AWS Opswork

224.   You need to upload an audio file and generate text file through Amazon EC2 worker instances, and you want both files in durable storage independent of size until text file is retrieved. Which is cost effective and scalable storage?

a) Multiple instance stores
b) Single Amazon S3 bucket
c) Multiple Amazon EBS volume with snapshots
d) Single Amazon Glacier vault

225.   An aerospace company has a track of GPS coordinates of spaceships. Coordinates are transmitted once every 5 seconds from each spaceship, and they want real-time processing of coordinates from multiple spaceships. Which service is helpful to implement data ingestion?

a) AWS Data Pipeline

b) AWS SQS
c) Amazon app stream
d) Amazon Kinesis

226.   A company wants to distribute content from the S3 bucket, and these content are accessible by some users. Distribution is down through CloudFront distribution. Which solution fulfills the requirement?

a) Use IAM policies for an underlying S3 bucket to restrict data
b) Create CloudFront signed URLs and then distribute these URLs to the users
c) Create IAM users for each user and provide access to bucket content
d) Use Create IAM groups for each set of users and then give access to the S3 bucket content

227.   A solution architect plans to design a stack-based model for its AWS resources and need a different stack for the different work environment. Which solution meets the requirements?

a) Use AWS OpsWork to define the different layer for your application
b) Define metadata for different layers in DynamoDB
c) Define metadata for different layers in RDS
d) Use AWS Config to define the different layers for your application

228.   How you give and manage permissions to a different type of users for API gateway?

a) Use IAM access keys to create sets of keys for different types of user
b) Use STS to manage the permission for different users
c) Use IAM policies to create different policies for different t type of users
d) Use AWS config tool to manage the permission for a different type of user

229.   A solution architect has a two-tier web application in 4 AZ within a region with ELB and auto-scaling, and they need that app will be available entirely in case of failure of any application AZ because it depends on synchronous replication at the database layer, and auto-scaling doesn't launch a new instance in other AZ. Which solution meet the above requirements?

a) Deploy in 4 regions using weighted round robin with an auto-scaling minimum set at 100% peak load per region
b) Deploy in 4 regions using weighted round robin with an auto-scaling minimum set at 25% peak load per region
c) Deploy in 5 AZ with an auto-scaling minimum set to handle 20% load per zone
d) Deploy in 5 AZ with an auto-scaling minimum set to handle a 25% load per zone

230. An organization needs their virtual machines on AWS cloud. How they import them to AWS cloud?

a) AWS import/export
b) DB migration Service
c) AWS Storage gateway
d) VM import/export

231. A solution architect design an architect for the organization in the primary and secondary region consist of an ELB and underlying EC2 for the scenario of disaster recovery. Which solution helpful to switchover when a primary region fails?

a) Use CloudTrail to detect the failure and then do a failover
b) Use a script to scan CloudWatch logs to detect the failure and then do the failover
c) Use CloudWatch metrics to detect the failure and then do the failover
d) Use Route53 Health Checks and then do a failover

232. How you encrypt all data in S3 at rest?

a) Enable MFA on the S3 bucket
b) Enable Server-side encryption on the S3 bucket
c) Use AWS Access Keys to encrypt the data
d) Use SSL certificates to encrypt data

233. Which AWS storage gateway configuration is used for backup an offsite data and this data is available for frequently access with low latency? The actual data size is 6-TB volume on-premises, and it increases to 300GB per year.

a) Gateway-Virtual Tape Library with snapshots to Amazon Glacier
b) Gateway-Virtual Tape Library with snapshots to Amazon S3
c) Gateway-Cached Volume with snapshots scheduled to Amazon S3
d) Gateway-stored Volume with snapshots scheduled to Amazon S3

234.   How a solution architect design an architect to host database server which can connect with internet only when database patches are needed during downloading otherwise it cannot connect to the internet?

a) Setup the database in the local data center and use a private gateway to connect the application to the database
b) Setup the database in public subnet with security group which only allows outbound traffic
c) Setup database in a private subnet which connects to the internet via a NAT instance
d) Setup the database in public subnet with security group which only allows inbound traffic

235.   An organization needs cost-effective, highly available, secure and scalable data layer to store user preferences data for an application which is used by a huge number of users. Each data size is 30 KB. Which solution meets the above requirements?

a) Use an Amazon Redshift cluster for managing the user preferences
b) Use Amazon Glacier to store the user data
c) Create DynamoDB table with required Read and Write capacity and use it as a data layer
d) Use Amazon S3 to store user data

236.   Consider your important data is in Amazon Aurora MySQL DB. As a solution architect in case of a disaster how you made data available in another region?

a) Create an EBS snapshot of underlying EBS volumes in Amazon Cluster and then copy them in another region
b) Make a copy of underlying EBS volumes in Amazon cluster in another region
c) Enable Multi-AZ for the Aurora database
d) Create Read Replica for the database

237.   As a solution architect which AWS service, you used as standard file interface for files across all Linux based instances.

   a) Consider Using AWS EFS
   b) Consider using AWS Amazon S3
   c) Consider using AWS Amazon glacier
   d) Consider Using AWS RDS

238.   As a solution architect, what is a modification you do in an Architecture to enhance security on AWS? An architecture contains web servers in public subnet which are accessed by the user over the internet and a database server in another public subnet.

   a) Consider Creating a private subnet and adding NAT instances to that subnet
   b) Consider moving web server in private subnet
   c) Consider moving database server in private subnet
   d) Consider moving both servers in private subnet

239.   Why SQS service is used for transcoding the video files which are sent from the on-premises system to AWS?

   a) SQS helps to facilitate horizontal scaling of encoding tasks
   b) SQS guarantees the order of messages
   c) SQS helps to facilitate vertical scaling of encoding task
   d) SQS synchronously provides transcoding output.

240.   A company has an application consist of EC2 instances in the Europe region, and they want resources quickly provided in another region in case of disaster. Which solution fulfills the above requirements? (choose 2)

   a) Copy the metadata for the EC2 instances to S3
   b) Copy the underlying EBS volumes to the destination region
   c) Create EBS snapshots and copy them to the destination region
   d) Create AMIs for underlying instances

241.   How you design an architect to extend on-premises infrastructure to AWS Cloud along with the communication of both environments over the internet?

a) Create a Virtual private gateway connection between the on-premises and the AWS environment
b) Create VPC peering connection between the on-premises and the AWS environment
c) Create an AWS direct connection between the on-premises and the AWS environment
d) Create VPN connection between the on-premises and AWS environment

242. If you want to use Redshift as a service and its data for the next two years continuously for researching purpose, then which cost-effective solution you used for the above condition?

a) Consider using Reserved instances for Redshift Cluster
b) Consider not using the cluster for Redshift nodes
c) Consider using on-demand instances for Redshift Cluster
d) Enabled automated backup

243. Which AWS service you used to shift your overall data storage to AWS cloud?

a) AWS RDS
b) AWS DynamoDB
c) AWS Redshift
d) AWS S3

244. How you scale your infrastructure hosted in AWS that contain two EC2 instances serving web-based application, an RDS enabled Multi-AZ and an Elastic Balancer in front of EC2 instances?

a) Add an auto scaling group to the setup
b) Enabled read replicas for AWS RDS
c) Add another ELB to setup
d) Add more EC2 instances to the setup

245. An organization has an architecture which contains an ELB in front of EC2 instances and AWS RDS as a database but due to a high number of read request database performance is not good. Which solution is best to choose to optimize performance?

a) Use DynamoDB to offload all reads. Settle the common read items in a separate table
b) Enable Multi-AZ to add a secondary read-only DB in another AZ
c) Use ElastiCache in front of Database
d) Use AWS CloudFront in front of the database

246.   An organization has an architect which contain two management web server with reserved EC2 instances along with EBS-backed root volumes and Multi-AZ RDs MySQL database for management and implementation. The traffic among instances is distributed through ELB. As a solution architect how you reduce the cost of this environment without affecting the availability of the system.

a) Consider not using Multi-AZ RDS for implementation database
b) Consider removing Elastic Load Balancer
c) Consider using Spot instances instead of reserved instances
d) Consider using on-demand instances instead of reserved instances

247.   As a solution architect, you need to propose an architect to construct some on-premises component to AWS cloud-like storage data layer with less administrative work. (choose 2)

a) Use RDS to store data
b) Use Amazon S3 to store data
c) Use DynamoDB to store data in tables
d) Use EC2 to host data on EBS volumes

248.   Consider files need to be transformed, but initially, they are stored in Amazon S3 and then spot EC2 instances transformed them quickly. Files submitted by special clients need to be transformed on highest priority. How you design such an architect?

a) Use a single SQS queue, so each message contains priority level, and by that priority, transformation instances polls the message
b) Use Route53 latency-based routing to send high priority task to closest transformation instances
c) Use a DynamoDB table with an attribute defining priority level, so instance scan the table and sorting the result by priority level

d) Use two SQS one with default priority and other is with high priority. So instances poll first high priority than the default priority

249. Consider a web application hosted on EC2 server with Public IP address which is mapped to domain names but due to some issue the server restarted and after that web application is not accessible via domain name. What was the reason behind this?

   a) The public IP address needs to be associated with ENI again
   b) The public IP address has changed after the instance was stopped and started
   c) The Route53 hosted zone needs to be restarted
   d) Network interface need to be initialized again

250. An application performs three functions uploading, processing and then publishing of audios. An application architecture contains EC2 instances to shift uploaded audio to S3 bucket, for publishing and processing EC2 worker are used and auto-scaling group for the EC2 worker. As an architect which AWS service need to add on in architecture to make it reliable

   a) Amazon SNS
   b) Amazon SES
   c) Amazon SQS
   d) Amazon CloudFront

251. Which is the most cost-effective storage type required by an organization which has an application running on EC2 Instance with 200 GB relational database and application is used infrequently with small spikes but not throughout the day?

   a) Amazon EBS general purpose SSD
   b) Amazon EBS provisioned IOPS SSD
   c) Amazon EFS
   d) Amazon EBS Throughput optimized HDD

252. Which AWS service is used by an application that required file storage which can share between Instances and extend the platform more easily?

   a) Amazon S3

b) Amazon EBS

c) Amazon EFS

d) Amazon EC2 instance

253. What type of storage is the most cost-effective in use by an organization to run service to provide backup for images and retrieval of images immediately although retrieval is infrequently accessed? The service also provides support to access thousands of images per customer.

a) Amazon S3 standard

b) Amazon EFS

c) Amazon Glacier with expedited retrievals

d) Amazon S3 Standard infrequent access

254. An organization required a solution to store and archive critical data, and they consider Amazon Glacier as the best choice, but they need that data must be delivered within 10 minutes of a retrieval request for this type of requirement which amazon glacier feature is best.

a) Expedited Retrieval

b) Standard Retrieval

c) Vault lock

d) Bulk Retrieval

255. Which solution is best to choose by a company to access the data that are pulled from the internet by a data processing application without placing bandwidth restriction on application traffic?

a) Attach VPC and add routes for 0.0.0.0/0

b) Deploy NAT instance in public subnet and add routes for 0.0.0.0/0

c) Launch NAT gateway and add routes for 0.0.0.0/0

d) Attach an internet gateway and add routes for 0.0.0.0/0

256. In the same duration when your application is scaling up and down multiple times, and you observe this through autoscaling event then which design is most suitable to reduce the cost with keeping its elasticity. (choose two best option)

a) Modify the auto scaling group termination policy to terminate new instances first
b) Modify the auto scaling group termination policy to terminate old instances first
c) Modify the CloudWatch Alarm period that provokes auto-scaling scale down policy
d) Modify auto scaling group cooldown timers.

257. In an organization, there is multiple application running from which one of the web application connects to Amazon RDS MYSQL DB running in VPC subnet with default ACL setting. In that application, the database must be accessible to the web server in the public cloud while the web server is accessible to the customers on an SSL connection then which design meets the above requirements. (choose 2)

a) Create DB server security group that allows HTTP port 80 inbound and specify source like a web server security group
b) Create DB server security group that allows MySQL port 3306 inbound and specify source like a web server security group
c) Create a network ACL on the web server's subnets, allow HTTP port 443 inbound and specify source 0.0.0.0/0
d) Create a web server security group that allows HTTPs port 443 inbound traffic from anywhere (0.0.0.0/0) and apply it to web servers.

258. An organization deployed the application in which read/write traffic to an S3 bucket is very high. Which method is best for maximizing the performance of Amazon S3.
a) Use the standard – IA storage class
b) Prefix each object name with current data
c) Prefix each object name with random strings
d) Enable versioning

259. To securely pass credentials to the application that calls AWS API's and deploy in Amazon EC2 than which method is used.

a) Embed API credentials into your applications
b) Pass API credential to the instance with instance user data.
c) Assign IAM roles to the EC2 instance
d) Store API credential as an object in Amazon S3

260. A company website is running on EC2 instance following with ELB load balancer. A company needs better website experience for the user because instance delivers various large files that are stored in Amazon EFS file system to avoid these file serving from the instance on user requests for these digital assets which way is better?

   a) Cache static content using cloud front
   b) Used reserved EC2 instance
   c) Resizing of image
   d) Move digital assets to Amazon Glacier.

261. A company needs a system to keep records, and these records are available for download for up to 5 months, and after that, it must be deleted, in which storage lifecycle policy is created for removing files after five months.

   a) Amazon EBS
   b) Amazon S3
   c) Amazon Glacier
   d) Amazon EFS

262. An organization is creating a large number of architectures for customers multiple times by using AWS resources, and they have an architecture diagram for each architecture, and they need a solution for automatically assigning resources to architecture. Which resource is used by the organization?

   a) AWS CloudFormation
   b) AWS CodeDeploy
   c) AWS CodeBuild
   d) AWS Beanstalk

263. Which security policy is used to encrypt data before writing to the disk?

   a) IAM access key
   b) API gateway with STS
   c) AWS KMS API
   d) AWS certificate manager

264. An organization need to store all its data in Amazon EBS volumes and want to be back up of data with durability over multiple Availability Zones. How you backup the volumes?

   a) Enable EBS volume encryption
   b) Create a script to copy data to an instance store
   c) Take regular EBS snapshots
   d) Replicate data across 2 EBS volumes

265. A broker performs exporting by transporting data from the transactional database into an S3 bucket in specific region and data can only be transported within a VPC according to security policy and its warehouse required to import data in Amazon Redshift cluster in their VPC at the same region. What steps will fulfill the security policy? (choose 2)

   a) Create and configure an Amazon S3 VPC endpoint
   b) Create a cluster Security group to allow Amazon Redshift Cluster to access Amazon S3
   c) Enable Amazon Redshift Enhanced VPC routing
   d) Create NAT gateway in a public subnet to allow Amazon Redshift Cluster to access Amazon S3

266. Which is the best option to enhance the performance of uploading a large number of files into Amazon S3?

   a) Use hexadecimal hash for suffix
   b) Use sequential ID for suffix
   c) Use hexadecimal hash for prefix
   d) Use sequential ID for suffix

267. An estate agency required a property file system to store data which can be accessed through EC2 instance. Which service is used for given scenario?

   a) AWS Glacier
   b) AWS EFS
   c) Amazon S3
   d) Amazon CloudFront

268. For sending and processing a significant amount of data sequentially which service is used?

   a) AWS SNS
   b) AWS ELB
   c) AWS Config
   d) AWS SQS FIFO

269. A company required a data store in the application which must continue and indicate JSON files. According to the above requirement which service is used?

   a) Amazon Redshift
   b) Amazon RDS
   c) Amazon DynamoDB
   d) Amazon ElastiCache

270. A company has a multi-language website on AWS by using CloudFront then how the configuration of Cloud Front would be done for caching incorrect data language. Language is specified in HTTP request like (http://d11111abcdef8.cloudfront.net/main.html?language=de).

   a) Serve dynamic content
   b) Cache objects at the origin
   c) Forward queries to the origin
   d) Based on query string parameter

271. An organization has an event for which registration is required, and they required to send messages on every signup of users. Which service is used?

   a) Amazon SNS
   b) Amazon SQS
   c) AWS lambda
   d) Amazon STS

272. An educational institute required shared service for hosting containers which are used for various AWS services on Amazon EC2 with other educational institutes. What type of solution is used to restrict data in such a way that one institute is not able to access other data?

   a) IAM roles for EC2 instance
   b) Security group rules
   c) IAM roles for the task
   d) IAM instance profile for EC2 instance

273. To summarize a vast amount of rows into column-wise by creating large datasets and want to create a report from these data sets then which storage service is required?

   a) Amazon EFS
   b) Amazon Redshift
   c) ElastiCache
   d) DynamoDB

274. An organization required an application for storing a session data. Which AWS storage is used? (choose 2)

   a) Storage Gateway
   b) DynamoDB
   c) ElastiCache
   d) Elastic Load Balancing

275. Students store images from university application that are uploaded by university and university required some security to avoid data loss. Which track they need to follow to prevent unintentional user action?

   a) Store data in S3 bucket and enable versioning.
   b) Store data on EC2 instance storage
   c) Store data in EBS volume and create snapshot once a week
   d) Store data in the different S3 bucket in a different region.

276. A company required data storage having 8TB of initial data storage capacity, the ability of database growth of 5GB per day and capability of 3 read replicas. Which data store meet the following requirement?

    a) Amazon S3
    b) Amazon Glacier
    c) Amazon Aurora
    d) DynamoDB

277. Which Amazon EBS volume type is used to host a database on EC2 with the support of 11000 IOPS?

    a) EBS Throughput Optimized HDD
    b) EBS cold HDD
    c) EBS general purpose SSD
    d) EBS provisioned IOPS SSD

278. The organization required to store log files for the various application in Amazon S3 bucket and want to keep that logs for a month for further testing purpose and then remove that log. Which feature will do this?

    a) Adding bucket policy on S3 bucket
    b) Enable CORS in S3 bucket
    c) Creating IAM policy for an S3 bucket
    d) Configure lifecycle rule on S3 bucket

279. Which AWS service is used to support application that uses NGINX and can modify at any time? (choose 2)

    a) AWS ELB
    b) AWS EBS
    c) AWS EC2
    d) AWS Elastic Beanstalk

280. To get the IP address of a resource which is accessed through a private subnet then which service this requirement fulfill?

a) Trusted Advisor
b) CloudTrial
c) VPC flow logs
d) Cloud Watch metrics

281. A company required a database for the two-tier application. The database should be durable, and change in the database does not result in downtime of the database. Which storage is best for the given scenario.

   a) AWS Aurora
   b) AWS S3
   c) AWS Redshift
   d) AWS DynamoDB

282. In company application, there is a Redshift cluster which contains 40 TB of data, and they need to put disaster recovery site in such a region which is 100 km away then which solution is helpful?

   a) Create a cloud formation template to restore the cluster in another region
   b) Take a copy of EBS volumes to S3 and then do cross region multiplication
   c) Enable cross region snapshots for Redshift cluster
   d) Enable cross availability zone snapshot for Redshift cluster.

283. Redshift is used by a company to store data, and they required internal IT security to encrypt that data for Redshift then which step should be taken?

   a) Use S3 encryption
   b) Use AWS KMS customer master key
   c) Use HTTP/ HTTPs for encryption
   d) Use SSL/TLS for encrypting data

284. A company needs block-level storage with data encryption. Which storage is used in this case?

   a) AWS Glacier
   b) AWS S3

c) AWS EFS
d) AWS EBS volumes

285. An organization required storage for batch processing activity that gives a throughput of max 500MiB/s. Which Storage is best?

a) EBS SSD
b) EBS Cloud Storage
c) EBS IOPS
d) EBS Throughput Optimized

286. An organization required a document sharing application with storage along with the automatic support of versioning so the administration can roll back the previous version and get back the deleted account of their employees. For these requirements organization use which AWS service?

a) Amazon Glacier
b) Amazon EBS
c) Amazon S3
d) Amazon EFS

287. A company required an application running in us-east-2 region with 4 EC2 instances operating all -east-2cat the same time. They have three availability zones in region us-east-2a, us-east-2b and us-east-2c. in case of unavailability of any availability zone then which deployment provide fault resistance? (choose two answers)

a) 2 EC2 Instances in us-east-2a, 2 EC2 Instances in us-east-2b and 2 EC2 Instances in us-east-2c
b) 4 EC2 Instances in us-east-2a, 2 EC2 Instance in us-east-2b and no EC2 Instances in us-east-2c
c) 4 EC2 Instances in us-east-2a, 4 EC2 Instance in us-east-2b and no EC2 Instances in us-east-2c
d) 1 EC2 Instances in us-east-2a, 1 EC2 Instance in us-east-2b and 2 EC2 Instances in us-east-2c

288. Which is the most cost-effective architecture used in an application to upload files and processed these files to extract metadata because this processing takes few seconds

per file and frequency of uploading the files in unpredictable, so there may be no update in an instance while the file is being uploaded?

a) Store the file in an EBS volume and then for processing it can be accessed by another EC2 instance.
b) For storing file use kinesis data delivery system and for processing use Lambda.
c) Store file in S3 bucket and use Amazon S3 event notification to request a Lambda function for processing.
d) Use an SQS queue for storage and use a fleet of EC2 Instance for accessing.

289.   Which RDS engine is used by a company that required to shift its database to AWS with replica delay of 80 milliseconds and a quadruple increase in the size of 20TB MySQL database of the company.

a) Oracle
b) Amazon Aurora
c) MySQL
d) Microsoft SQL Server

290.   For creating a web server and worker environment which AWS service is used in Solution Architect.

a) AWS Lambda
b) AWS Elastic Beanstalk
c) AWS Batch
d) Amazon Lightsail

291.   A company required access to data from another AWS account in the same region. Which step needs to be following?

a) Establish NAT instance between both accounts
b) Use VPC peering between both accounts
c) Use NAT gateway between both accounts
d) Use VPN between both accounts.

292. An organization needs to use NAT gateway as they are using NAT Instance then which step is best to choose?

a) Host NAT in private subnet
b) Convert NAT instance into NAT gateway
c) Use NAT instance along with NAT gateway
d) Migrate NAT instance to a NAT gateway and host it in public subnet

293. An institute required an application which contains EC2 instances in multiple AZ's behind ELB, launching of EC2 instances via autoscaling group and NAT instance to download updates from the internet. Which element is a barrier to architecture?

a) An ELB
b) NAT Instance
c) Auto-scaling group
d) The EC2 instance

294. A company gets 1000 of requests per second through its API, and they want to manage it cost-effectively. Which solution is best?

a) Using API gateway along with AWS Lambda
b) Use ElastiCache along with API
c) Use API gateway along with backend service as it is
d) Use CloudFront along with API backend service as it is

295. An organization needs a database to perform a vast amount of reading and writes operation then which storage is best?

a) EBS SSD
b) EBS Cloud Storage
c) EBS Provisioned IOPS
d) EBS Throughput Optimized

296. When you store data in S3, then you need to store its metadata and required to be indexed. Which storage is used to store metadata?

a) Amazon DynamoDB
b) Amazon Aurora

c) AWS RDS
d) AWS S3

297. An organization backup their EBS volumes with the help of EBS snapshots. The organization required these snapshot to be available in another region. Which option suits best?

a) Create a snapshot and copy it in another region
b) Copy snapshot to an S3 bucket and enable cross-region replication for the bucket
c) Copy the EBS snapshot to an EC2 instance in another region
d) Directly create a snapshot in another region

298. A company has its advertising drive hosted on EC2 instance due to starts within a week. Its mandatory for management to give surety that in case of traffic growth no problem detected in performance. Which requirement is best to choose?

a) Configured static scaling for auto-scaling group
b) Configure scheduled scaling for auto-scaling group
c) Configure step scaling for the auto scaling group
d) Configured dynamic scaling and use target tracking scaling group

299. An institute has an application and administration required some aspects like notification sending when read requests go above the 500 requests per second; notification sends when latency go above the 5 seconds and for sensitive data an API activity should be monitored. Further, this application is consist of EC2 instances which sit behind an ELB. Choose any two solutions which fulfill the requirement. (choose 2)

a) Use the CloudWatch log to monitor the API activity
b) Use custom log software to monitor the latency and read requests to the ELB
c) Use CloudTrail to monitor the API activity
d) Use CloudWatch metrics for the metrics that need to be monitored as per requirement and set up an activity to send out a notification when metric reaches the set threshold limit

300. An organization has an application on AWS account and required monitoring of API activity for all-region and also need auditing of the future region as well. Which solution is best?

a) Create CloudTrail for each region. Use CloudFormation to enable the trail in all region
b) Create CloudTrail for each region. Use AWS Config to enable the trail in all region
c) Ensure CloudTrail for each region, then enable for each future region
d) Ensure that CloudTrail trail is enabled for all region

301.   The company needs an iSCSI device, and legacy application required local storage. Which storage is best?

a) Configure the Simple Storage Service
b) Configure Amazon Glacier
c) Configured Storage Gateway Stored Volume
d) Configured Storage Gateway Cached Volume

302.   A client wants to access its S3 bucket through the EC2 instance in private subnet, and also want that traffic does not traverse to the internet then which solution you will choose to fulfill requirements?

a) Internet gateway
b) VPC endpoint
c) NAT Instance
d) NAT gateway

303.   Which solution is best to choose for scaling proxy and backend instances correctly in the case when your application is not able to scale appropriately while creating an application on EC2 instances after a classic ELB and EC2 proxy is used for content management to backend instances? (select 2)

a) Use auto-scaling for backend instances
b) Replace the Classic ELB with application ELB
c) Use auto-scaling for proxy servers
d) Use application ELB for both front-end and backend instances

304. A channel website hosted on AWS faced a massive amount of traffic over the next couple of months. In case of a disaster in the application which solution is best to choose for recovery from disasters.

    a) Use CloudFormation to create backup resources in another AZ
    b) Use ELB to divert traffic to an infrastructure hosted in another AZ
    c) Use Route53 to route to the static website
    d) Use ELB to redirect traffic to an infrastructure hosted in another region

305. To host a static website of your domain like ipspecialist.net in AWS, you required surety that traffic is appropriately scaled. Which solution is best (select 2)

    a) Place EC2 instance after ELB
    b) Enter the NS record from Route53 in domain registrar
    c) Host static site on EC2 instance
    d) Use Route53 with the static website in S3

306. A database receives a lot of queries hosted by RDS service in AWS, and this will become a barrier in the application. Which solutions do not make the database a barrier to performance?

    a) Set up an ELB in front of the database
    b) Set up an ElastiCache in front of a database.
    c) Set up an SNS in front of the database
    d) Setup CloudDistribution in front of a database.

307. A database is made into a production database hosted by RDS service in AWS and also required high availability. Which step is used to achieve requirements?

    a) Use read replica feature to create another instance of DB in another region
    b) Use read replica feature to create another instance of DB in another AZ
    c) Use Multi-AZ for the RDS instance to ensure that a secondary database is created in another AZ
    d) Use Multi-AZ for the RDS instance to ensure that a secondary database is created in another region

308. An organization required to host application and database layer in AWS with the help of using subnets in a VPC. Which architectural design is best for a given condition?

a) Use public subnet for the web tier and a private subnet for the database layer
b) Use private subnet for the web tier and a private subnet for the database layer
c) Use public subnet for the web tier and a public subnet for the database layer
d) Use private subnet for the web tier and a public subnet for the database layer

309. The client required its user's clickstream data on the website for analyzing. He wants a sequence of pages as well as ads clicked by their user. Now, this data will be used in modifying page layouts as user click through the site to increase stickiness and advertising click through. Which solution is best to do captioning and analyzing of data?

a) Write click events directly to Amazon RDS and then analyze it with SQL
b) Publish web clicks by session to an Amazon SQS queue and then send an event to AWS RDS for further processing
c) Publish web clicks by session to an Amazon SNS queue and then send an event to AWS DynamoDB for further processing
d) Push web clicks by session to Amazon Kinesis and analyze behavior using Kinesis workers

310. An IT company infrastructure consists of a considerable number of machines which sends logs after every 2 minutes, and they want that this analyzing of data would be done later. Which solutions fit best to resolve this?

a) Launch an EC2 instance with enough EBS volumes to store logs for further processing
b) Use cloud trail to store all logs and analyze them later
c) Use Kinesis Firehose with S3 to take logs and store them in S3 for further processing
d) Launch an Elastic Beanstalk application to take the job of processing logs

311. A client wants access to upload some video files on monthly bases in S3 bucket with the help of application hosted in AWS. Which is the best possible way?

a) Create an IAM role to provide access for a monthly duration
b) Create an IAM bucket policy to provide access for a monthly duration

c) Create an S3 bucket policy to provide access for the monthly duration

d) Create a pre-signed URL for each profile which will last for the monthly duration.

312. An organization required batch processing for which they are thinking to use Docker containers and necessary container orchestration tools. They want batch processing of both critical and non-critical data. Which suits best in a cost-effective way for the given demand?

a) Use Docker for container orchestration and the combination of spot and reserved instances for underlying instance.

b) Use ESC orchestration and reserved instance for all underlying instance

c) Use Kubernetes for container orchestration and reserved instance for all underlying instance

d) Use ECS for container orchestration and the combination of spot and reserved instances for underlying instance.

313. The client wants to archive data of 4 TB, and he agreed with stakeholder for 7 hour retrieval time. Which storage is the most cost-effective?

a) AWS EBS volumes

b) AWS Snowball

c) AWS S3 Standard

d) AWS Glacier

314. Which routing policy is best to choose when you have 2-6 web servers, and you want to use Route53 to route the user traffic toward random web servers when they request for basic web applications?

a) Latency

b) Multivalue answer

c) Simple

d) Weighted

315. A managed database to perform underlying queries which database is best to choose?

a) AWS RDS
b) AWS Redshift
c) AWS Aurora
d) AWS S3

316. An organization wants to test a significant amount of IoT enabled devices, and they want this device to do streaming of data every second. Which service is used to collect and analyze streams in real time?

a) Use SQL to store data
b) Use SNS to store data
c) Use EMR to store data
d) Use AWS Kinesis Streams to process and analyze data.

317. The organization required storage of 70TB of data, and then data consist in database layer after exporting with the help of AWS Snowball. The database should query from a business intelligence application, and each item is of 100 KB in size. Which storage is best for the data layer.

a) AWS RDS
b) AWS Aurora
c) AWS Redshift
d) AWS S3

318. When you create a stream of EBS volume, how you encrypt the data at rest on the volume?

a) Use KMS to generate encryption keys which can be used to encrypt the volume
b) Use EBS snapshot to encrypt the requests
c) Create SSL certificate and attach it to the EBS volume
d) Use CloudFront in front of EBS volume to encrypt data.

319. If your organization has multiple EC2 instances in AWS and you want to monitor the states of these instances as well as record the change in the state then which solution you used to achieve this? (Choose 2)

a) Use AWS Lambda to store a change record in DynamoDB table
b) Use CloudWatch logs to store the state change of instances
c) Use CloudWatch events to monitor the state changes of the event
d) Use SQL to trigger a record to be added to a DynamoDB table

320. An organization have instances and want to download updates in instances from the internet. Instances are hosted on the private subnet in a VPC. Which solution used by the organization efficiently and securely?

a) Use NAT gateway to allow the instances in the private subnet to download the updates
b) Create a new public subnet and move instances to that subnet
c) Create VPC link to the internet to allow the instances in private subnet to download the updates
d) Create a new EC2 instance to download the updates separately and then push them to required instances

321. What type of EBS volume is best to store cold data at low cost?

a) EBS Cloud Storage
b) EBS Provisioned IOPS
c) Cold HDD
d) EBS Throughput Optimized

322. The application is hosted in AWS, and it has user uploading files and downloads these files later with the help of public URL. Which design will you choose according to requirements?

a) Use Amazon Glacier to host the files because it is the cheapest storage
b) Have EBS volumes hosted on EC2 instances to store the files
c) Use EBS snapshots attached to EC2 instances to store the files
d) Use Amazon S3 to host the files

323. For hosting a web application, you have two EC2 instances one is in public subnet, and other will host an Oracle database. In what way you will take a step for a secure connection between them? (choose 2)

a) Create a database security group and ensure that the web server's security group allows incoming access
b) Ensure that database security group allows incoming traffic from 0.0.0.0/0
c) Place the EC2 instances with Oracle database in a separate private subnet
d) Place the EC2 instance with Oracle database in the same public subnet as the web server for faster communication

324. In what way EC2 instance which is hosted in java based application securely access DynamoDB table when it is currently serving production users?

a) Use KMS keys with right permission to interact with DynamoDB and assign it to EC2 instance
b) Use IAM access group with correct permission to interact with DynamoDB and assign it to EC2 instance
c) Use IAM roles with right permission to interact with DynamoDB and assign it to EC2 instance
d) Use IAM Access keys with right permission to interact with DynamoDB and assign it to EC2 instance

325. An institute wants to construct a web application on AWS to store session data. Which service is used to fulfill the need?

a) AWS RDS
b) AWS Redshift
c) AWS ElastiCache
d) AWS ELB

326. When an application interacts with DynamoDB, and when any changes occur in DynamoDB table a quick entry is made to associating application. In what way you achieve this? (choose 2)

a) Trigger a Lambda function to create an associated entry in the application as soon as DynamoDB streams are modified
b) Setup Cloudwatch logs to monitor the DynamoDB table for changes and then With the help of AWS SQS send changes to the application
c) Setup Cloudwatch to monitor the DynamoDB table for changes and then trigger Lambda function to send changes to the application

d) Use DynamoDB streams to track the changes to DynamoDB table

327. An organization wants to move their application form on-premises to AWS. An application contains web instances, worker instances and Rabbit-MQ for messaging purpose. Which architecture is best to choose for shifting?
a) Make use of AWS Redshift to store messages
b) Make use of AWS RDS to store messages
c) Make use of AWS SQS to manage the massages
d) Continue using rabbit-MQ. Host it on a separate EC2 instance.

328. An organization has RDS MySQL database in an application, but due to some issues in the database, they are deciding to use separate reporting layer for querying part. Which step is used to choose to meet the requirement?

a) Make use of Read replicas to set up a secondary read-only database
b) Make use of Read replicas to setup a secondary read and write database
c) Make use of Multi-AZ to set up a secondary database in another region
d) Make use of Multi-AZ to set up a secondary database in another Availability Zone

329. An institute required application logs to be stored in S3 bucket for a temporary period after that logs will be deleted. Which solution meets the above requirement?

a) Use an IAM policy to manage the deletion
b) Create a corn job to detect the stale logs and delete them accordingly
c) Use S3 lifecycle policy to manage the deletion
d) Use bucket policy to manage the deletion

330. A company had an application to process sensitive data running on EC2 and stored them in Amazon S3. IT team of an organization wants secure internet connectivity to Amazon S3 so that information is not accessible over the internet. Which solution fulfills the requirement?

a) Access data through a VPN connection
b) Access data through NAT gateway
c) Access data through a VPC endpoint for Amazon S3
d) Access data through an internet gateway.

331. In what way you should be able to access Redshift cluster in AWS?

    a) Change the encryption key associated with the cluster
    b) Ensure the cluster is created in the right region
    c) Ensure the cluster is created in the right availability zone
    d) Change the security group for the cluster

332. In what way you improve your architecture if users face extreme slowness in some region in accessing an EC2 instance when the EC2 instance is accessible by users globally?

    a) Add Route53 health checks to improve the performance
    b) Place EC2 instance behind CloudFront
    c) Change the instance type to a higher instance type
    d) Add more EC2 instance to support load

333. How you make your NAT gateway highly available for your private instances?

    a) Create NAT gateway in another region
    b) Create another NAT gateway and place it after an ELB
    c) Use Auto Scaling groups to scale the NAT gateway
    d) Create NAT gateway in another availability zone

334. An organization has an application which need fully managed data storage compatible with MySQL database. Which database should you need to choose?

    a) AWS Redshift
    b) AWS Aurora
    c) AWS RDS
    d) AWS DynamoDB

335. An institute is planning to design online library system application for students on EC2 instances running in auto scaling group across Multiple AZ in VPC after ELB application load balancer. In application read and write data of students in the database cluster. Which VPC design you choose to meet the requirement along with that the

database is not accessible from the internet, but database cluster must obtain software patches from the internet.

a) Public subnets for the application tier and NAT gateway, and private subnets for the database cluster
b) Private subnets for the database cluster and private subnets for the application tier
c) Private subnets for both the application tier and database cluster
d) Public subnets for the application tier and private subnets for database cluster and NAT gateway

336. Consider you need to upload an image in S3 through the mobile application with the use of existing web server because of the load in uploading an image. In what way you achieve the requirement.

a) Use ECS container to upload an image
b) Create a secondary S3 bucket and then use AWS lambda to sync the content to primary bucket
c) Upload the image to SQL and then push them to S3 bucket
d) Use pre-signed URLs instead to upload an image.

337. An organization uses a MySQL database hosted by AWS RDS. This database is further used for experiencing a high amount of read/write operation and for production purposes. Which EBS volume is used for this requirement?

a) EBS Cloud Storage
b) Cold HDD
c) EBS Throughput Optimized
d) EBS Provisioned IOPS

338. An organization has an on-premises virtual machine which is placed behind an on-premises load balanced solution. What is the solution you used to choose in case of virtual machine become unhealthy it is taken out of the rotation?

a) Move solution to AWS and use a Classic Load Balancer
b) Move solution to AWS and use Network Load Balancer
c) Use Route53 health checks to monitor the endpoints
d) Move solution to AWS and use Application Load Balancer

339. What step do you follow to analyzed logs in real time to detect any threat in web servers?

   a) Upload logs to Amazon Kinesis and then analyze logs accordingly
   b) Upload logs to the Glacier and then analyze the logs accordingly
   c) Upload all logs to SQL and then use EC2 instances to scan the logs
   d) Upload logs to Cloudtrail and then analyze logs accordingly

340. If an organization want well-architected framework and they have already an architecture in AWS contains a couple of EC2 instances located in us-east-2a, launching of EC2 instances via auto scaling group and launch EC2 behind a Classic ELB. What is the solution which meets to architect well?

   a) Add additional EC2 instance to us-east-2a
   b) Convert classic ELB to an application ELB
   c) Add or spread existing instances across multiple Availability Zones
   d) Add Auto Scaling Group

341. In organization customers are allowed to upload images in an S3 bucket then EC2 instances picked images and process it after that it will be stored to another S3 bucket. Which data store is ideal to store metadata of these images?

   a) AWS SQS
   b) AWS S3
   c) AWS Redshift
   d) AWS DynamoDB

342. How you quickly provide development application environment consist of a web and database layer?

   a) Create reserved instances and install the web and database component.
   b) Use AWS Lambda to create the web components and AWS RDS for database layer.
   c) Create Spot instances and install the web and database components
   d) Use Elastic Beanstalk to provision the environment quickly.

343. Which is the best ideal storage for file systems across a group of instances?

   a) AWS EBS volumes
   b) AWS EFS
   c) AWS S3
   d) AWS Glacier

344. Which is the most cost-effective storage to store images that are not frequently accessed while images and thumbnails images stores in S3 initially and thumbnails images need to be available for quick download?

   a) Amazon EFS
   b) Amazon S3 Standard
   c) Amazon Glacier with expedited retrievals
   d) Amazon S3 Standard Infrequent Access

345. You need to create an EC2 instance which will be used by the clients on the internet so it must have complete access over the internet. This instance is added to the VPC which was created from scratch. Which will fulfill the requirements?

   a) Deploy NAT instances in a public subnet and add routes for 0.0.0.0/0
   b) Attach a VPC endpoint and add routes for 0.0.0.0/0
   c) Launch a NAT gateway and add routes for 0.0.0.0/0
   d) Attach an Internet gateway and add routes for 0.0.0.0/0

346. When do you observe that EC2 instances are not scaling up according to the need of application as EC2 instances launched on AWS via auto scaling group then what measures you need to take for expected scaling?

   a) Ensure that the instances are placed across multiple Availability Zones
   b) Ensure that the right metrics are being used to trigger the scale out
   c) Ensure that the instances are placed across multiple regions
   d) Ensure that ELB health checks are being used

347. An organization has an application on which a large number of users are expected with 600 reads and writes per second, and that application is hosted on AWS to write images in S3 bucket. In which way you maximize the performance of Amazon S3?

   a) Use the standard – IA storage class
   b) Prefix each object name with current data
   c) Prefix each object name with random strings
   d) Enable Versioning

348. If in the infrastructure of the organization code of template needs to be created for the use of providing the same set of resources in another region in case of a disaster in the primary region then through which AWS service they will achieve that target?

   a) AWS Codebuild
   b) AWS Codedeploy
   c) AWS Beanstalk
   d) AWS CloudFormation

349. In case of a disaster how we effectively managed the sets of EBS volume using the existing AWS services?

   a) Use EBS snapshots to create volumes in another availability zone
   b) Create a script to copy EBS volume to another availability zone
   c) Use EBS snapshots to create volumes in another region
   d) Create a script to copy the EBS volume to another region

350. A web distribution in the organization is hosted by AWS CloudFront service. An application which is using web distribution now falls under the scope of PCI compliance. What step should need to be taken to meet the compliance objective? (choose 2)

   a) Enable Cache in CloudFront
   b) Enable VPC Flow logs
   c) Capture requests which are sent to the CloudFront API
   d) Enable CloudFront access logs

351.   An institute wants to host subscription service in AWS so the student can subscribe to the same and get the notification on new updates of this service. Which service fulfill the requirements?

   a) Use SNS service to send notification
   b) Use AWS DynamoDB streams to send the notification
   c) Use SQS service to send the notification
   d) Host an EC2 instance and use the rabbit MQ service to send notification

352.   An organization has a group of EC2 instances hosted in AWS and need to be prepared about disaster recovery procedure in case of a disaster in what way you will reduce the effect of disaster?

   a) Use CloudFront in front of the EC2 instances
   b) Use AMIs to recreate the EC2 instances in another region
   c) Place an ELB in front of EC2 instances
   d) Use auto-scaling to ensure the minimum number of instances are always running

353.   If you want to make sure that all data to and from Redshift cluster does not go through the internet because of security reason. What will be the solution you choose to achieve this?

   a) Create NAT gateway to route the traffic
   b) Create VPN connection to ensure that traffic does not flow through the internet
   c) Enable Amazon Redshift enhanced VPC routing
   d) Create NAT instance to route the traffic

354.   An organization wants to shift a set of Hyper-V machines and VMware virtual machine to AWS cloud then how we move these resources to AWS cloud?

   a) Use AWS Config tools
   b) Use AWS migration tools
   c) DB migration utility
   d) Use the VM import tools

355.   An organization wants to store datasets in the equivalent block storage device on AWS same as on Linux based instances on their on-premises infrastructure. Which storage device you recommend them to use for that purpose?

   a) AWS RDS
   b) AWS S3
   c) AWS EBS
   d) AWS EFS

356.   An institute wants to shift their IT jobs setup in C# programming language to AWS. In AWS how IT-related jobs are hosted?

   a) Use Aws S3 to store jobs and then run them on demand
   b) Use AWS config function with C# for IT jobs
   c) Use AWS DynamoDB to store the jobs and then run them according to demand
   d) Use AWS Lambda function with C# for IT jobs

357.   Which is the most efficient way to monitor all the activity of AWS resources hosted on AWS cloud?
   a) Use AWS Inspector to inspect all of the resources in your account
   b) Use the AWS CloudTrail to monitor all API activity
   c) Use VPC Flow logs to monitor all activity in your VPC
   d) Use the AWS Trusted Advisor to monitor all of your resources.

358.   Which storage is ideal storage to perform SQL queries, integration with existing business intelligence and with high concurrency workload that includes reading and writing all columns of a small number of record at a time/ (choose 2)

   a) AWS RDS
   b) AWS Aurora
   c) AWS S3
   d) AWS Redshift

359.   In what way you cost-effectively use Redshift cluster?

   a) Use Spot instances for the underlying nodes in the cluster

b) Ensure that Cloudwatch metric are disabled
c) Ensure that unnecessary manual snapshots of the cluster are deleted
d) Ensure VPC Enhanced Routing is enabled

360.   Two companies have the same set of resources hosted in AWS VPC, one is the parent company, and the other is Child Company. How can the resources in VPC of the parent company access the resources in VPC of Child Company?

a) Use VPC peering to peer both VPCs
b) Establish a NAT instance to establish communication across VPCs
c) Establish a NAT gateway to establish communication across VPCs
d) Use VPC connection to peer both VPCs

361.   How you set up your application for better fault tolerance when its architect consists EC2 instance in a single AZ behind and ELB and a NAT instance which is used to ensure that instance can download updates from the internet? (choose 2)

a) Add more instances in another availability zone
b) Add more instances in existing availability zone
c) Add another ELB for more fault tolerance
d) Add an Auto Scaling Group to setup

362.   An organization is facing short of storage on their on-premises infrastructure, and they want any quick solution in AWS. In what way they extend their infrastructure to AWS?

a) Organization start using Amazon S3
b) Organization start using Gateway-Cached Volumes
c) Organization start using Amazon Glacier
d) Organization start using Stored Gateway Volumes

363.   In institute teacher uploads lectures daily and they need such type of durable storage in which any user is not able to delete any documentation and document is stored securely. Which storage is fulfilled above requirement?

a) Store data in two S3 buckets in different AWS regions
b) Store data in an EBS volume and create snapshots once a week

c) Store data on EC2 instance storage
d) Store data in S3 bucket and enable versioning

364. An organization needs a relational database with initial storage of 5TB, and they gradually grow by 7GB per day. To support this huge traffic, they need 8 read replicas to handle the database reads. Which database is best for given requirements?

a) Amazon S3
b) DynamoDB
c) Amazon Glacier
d) Amazon Aurora

365. A university has an application of library in which objects delivers from S3 to students and students from all over the world have access to these objects but some students across the globe complaining about the slow response. Which solution helps in a cost-effective way to ensure that students will get an optimal response from the S3 object?

a) Ensure S3 transfer acceleration is enabled to ensure that all students get desired response times
b) Place S3 bucket behind the CloudFront distribution
c) Use S3 replication to replicate the objects to regions closest to the users
d) Place an ELB in front of S3 to distribute the load across S3

366. A coaching center needs a messaging system in AWS which maintain the order of messages as well as not duplicate any message. Which AWS service meet the need?

a) AWS SWF
b) AWS SNS
c) AWS SQS FIFO
d) AWS ELB

367. Which AWS service can make application stateless and scale it according to the demand?

a) AWS SQS

b) AWS S3

c) AWS DynamoDB

d) AWS Lambda

368. Which architecture is most fault tolerant in case of a set of EC2 instances host on AWS cloud that forms a web server farm which provides services for accessing a web application to the user on the internet? (choose 2)

a) Use Auto-scaling to distribute traffic

b) Ensure instances are placed in separate availability zones

c) Use an AWS Load Balancer to distribute the traffic

d) Ensure instances are placed in separate regions

369. An organization required an application which is not critical and can start its operation after an interruption. The application is on EC2 instance, and its function is to process the logs. Which is the cost-effective solution to meet the above requirements?

a) Use spot instances for underlying EC2 instance

b) Use reserved instances for underlying EC2 instance

c) Use S3 as an underlying data layer

d) Use Provisioned IOPS for underlying EBS volumes

370. Which is the most efficient and best way to make an S3 bucket with searching capabilities for stored logs? (choose 2)

a) Load data in Glacier

b) Load data in Amazon Elastic Search

c) Load data in storage gateway

d) Use an AWS Lambda function which gets triggered whenever data is added to the S3 bucket

371. Which solution is best to choose to deploy batch processing application in AWS? (choose 2)

a) Deploy image as an Amazon ECS task

b) Copy batch processing application to an ECS container
c) Deploy the container behind ELB
d) Create Docker image of your batch processing application

372. In an organization, there is multiple application running from which one of the web application connects to Amazon RDS MYSQL DB running in VPC subnet with default ACL setting. In that application, the database must be accessible to the web server in the public cloud while the web server is accessible to the customers on an SSL connection then which design meets the above requirements. (choose 2)

a) Create DB server security group that allows HTTP port 80 inbound and specify source like a web server security group
b) Create DB server security group that allows MySQL port 3306 inbound and specify source like a web server security group
c) Create a network ACL on the web server's subnets, allow HTTP port 443 inbound and specify source 0.0.0.0/0
d) Create a web server security group that allows HTTPs port 443 inbound traffic from anywhere (0.0.0.0/0) and apply it to web servers.

373. An organization architecture consists of two infrastructure (primary and secondary) hosted in AWS, and both infrastructures contain ELB, Auto Scaling, and EC2 resources. How we configured Route53 in case of failure of primary infrastructure?

a) Configure a multi-answer routing policy
b) Configure primary routing policy
c) Configure failover routing policy
d) Configure a weighted routing policy

374. An organization need provisions test environment in a short duration and also have the ability to tear them down quickly in cost optimization. How we meet the requirements?

a) Use IAM policies for provisioning the resources and tearing them down accordingly
b) Use a custom script to create and tear down the resources
c) Use auto scaling groups to provide the resources on demand
d) Use cloud formation templates to provision the resources accordingly

375.   Which service provides self-manage database environment?

a) Use Dynamo DB service
b) Use AWS RDS
c) Create an EC2 instance and install database service accordingly
d) Use Aws Aurora

376.   An organization shifts its 10TB MySQL database to AWS with the expectation of an increase in size firmly. Which RDS engine fulfill the need?

a) Oracle
b) Amazon Aurora
c) MySQL
d) Microsoft SQL server

377.   If the client wants the 60Mbpos direct connection to its AWS service then which service is helpful?

a) Internet gateway
b) VPC
c) Virtual private gateway
d) Direct connection

378.   Which storage is the most cost-effective storage to store data for long-term and make the data available upon request although they will never be accessed?

a) AWS S3
b) AWS Glacier
c) AWS import/export
d) EBS volumes

379.   To serve dynamic transaction-based content, an organization need a two-tier web application. Data-tier uses as an online transactional process. Which service helps the web tier to be elastic and scalable?

a) Elastic Load Balancing, Amazon RDS with MultiAZ and Amazon S3
b) Amazon EC2, Amazon DynamoDB, and Amazon S3
c) Amazon DynamoDB, Elastic Load Balancing, and Amazon S3
d) Elastic Load Balancing, Amazon EC2 instance, and Auto-Scaling

380. Consider launching an instance in a VPC the instance security group is configured in such a way that it allows SSH from any IP address and deny all outbound traffic and the instance has also launched in VPC, so it has network ACL configured which allow inbound traffic and denies all outbound traffic. How you allow SSH to access the instance?

a) Outbound network ACL needs to be configured to allow outbound traffic
b) Both outbound security group and outbound network ACL need to modify to allow outbound traffic
c) Outbound security group need to be configured to allow outbound traffic
d) Nothing needs to be configured; you can access it from any IP address using SSH

381. If we want to store some documents in Amazon web services and the documents should be version controlled. Which is the ideal choice in this case?

a) Amazon EBS
b) Amazon S3
c) Amazon Glacier
d) Amazon EFS

382. If an application comprises of an EC2 Instance hosting a web application and application is connected with AWS RDS database. Chose any one which can be used to guarantee that the database layer is highly accessible?

a) Create another EC2 Instance in another Availability zone and host a replica of the web server
b) Create another EC2 Instance in another Availability zone and host a replica of the database
c) Enable Multi-AZ for the AWS RDS Database
d) Enable Read Replica for the AWS RDS Database

383. A client wants to upload files to an S3 bucket which was currently accepted by an application. Every file name for each uploaded file is stored in a DynamoDB table. How can this be achieved? Select any two.

   a) Use AWS cloudwatch to probe for any S3 event
   b) Add the cloud watch event to the DynamoDB table streams section
   c) Add an event with notification sends to Lambda
   d) Create an AWS Lambda function to insert the required entry for each uploaded files

384. An organization is currently running MySQL instance and wants to migrate to AWS.

Requirements are as follows
   a) Replication lag to be kept under 100 milliseconds
   b) Ability to support an initial size of 5TB
   c) Ability to allow the database to double in size

Which of the following meets these requirements?
   a) Amazon Aurora
   b) Oracle
   c) Microsoft SQL server
   d) MySQL

385. As a solution architect, you required to host a static website in AWS for an organization. Find an easy and cost-effective way from the following.
   a) Use S3 website hosting to host the website
   b) Create an ec2 instance, install the web server and then have the site setup
   c) Use elastic beanstalk to host the website
   d) Use cloudformatin templates to have the website setup
386. If an application itself did not have a high usage ratio, it currently wants to have a database hosted in AWS. In future, the database will be hosted on an EC2 instance. Reads and writes on the database would be lowest. What would be the most suitable storage type in this case?

a) Amazon EBS general purpose SSD
b) Amazon EFS
c) Amazon EBS provisioned IOPS SSD
d) Amazon EBS Throughput Optimized

387. An organization has an application which needs to have the file stored in AWS.

Requirement

Have the ability to mounted on various Linux EC2 instances.

Which is the ideal storage service in this case?

a) Amazon EC2 instance store
b) Amazon S3
c) Amazon EFS
d) Amazon EBS

388. A user upload images to an S3 bucket. In the initial stage, images will be downloaded frequently but after some time process is too slow, the image might only be accessed one time in a week and its retrieval time also minimize. Find any cost-effective solution, select any 2 answers

a) Create a lifecycle policy to transfer the object to S3-Standard storage after a certain duration of time
b) Create a lifecycle policy to transfer the object to S3-infrequent access storage after a certain duration of time
c) Store the object in the S3-Standard storage
d) Store the object in Amazon Glacier

389. An organization has lots of data, and they want to store their corporate documents. Another organization suggests them to use Amazon Glacier. From the following services which one is best for this case?

a) Using standard retrieval
b) Using bulk retrieval
c) Using expedited retrieval
d) Defining a vault lock

390. Kubernetes is required in an organization they use it as an orchestration tool for their application containers, and the fully managed solution is also needed. In this case what would be bets service?

a) AWS EKS
b) AWS Lambda
c) AWS API Gateway
d) AWS ELB

391. In an organization, an employ uses Auto-scaling to maintain the performance of his web application. How can he ensure that this activity has sufficient time to stabilize without executing another scaling action?

a)   Disable cloudwatch alarm till the application stabilizes
b)   Enable the auto scaling cross zone balancing feature
c)   Increase the auto scaling cooldown timer value
d)   Modify the instance user data property with a timeout interval

392. An organization hosts a very popular web application which is connected to an Amazon RDS MySQL DB instance running in a private VPC subnet created with default ACL settings. The IT Security department has identified a DDoS attack from a suspecting IP. How can you protect the subnets from attacks?

a)   Change the outbound NACL to deny access from the suspect IP
b)   Change the inbound NACL to deny access from the suspect IP
c)   Change the outbound security group to deny access from the suspect IP
d)   Change the inbound security group to deny access from the suspect IP

393. An organization is planning to allow their users to upload and read objects from an S3 bucket because of this read and write traffic will be huge. How can you maximize amazon S3 performance?

a)   Enable versioning on the S3 bucket
b)   Prefix each object name with the current data
c)   Use the standard IA storage class
d)   Prefix each object name with a random string

394. An EC2 instance setup wants to host an application in AWS which will make API calls to the simple storage service. Find the ideal path for application to access the simple storage service?

    a) Create and assign an IAM role to the EC2 instance
    b) Embed the API credentials into your application
    c) Store API credentials as an object in a separate Amazon S3 bucket
    d) Pass API credentials to the instance using instance user data

395. An organization uploaded videos to an S3 bucket, and they need to provide access to the employee to view same. Find the best way to do it.

    a)   Use AWS Lambda function to deliver the content to users
    b)   Use API gateway with S3 bucket as the source
    c)   Use CloudFront with the S3 bucket as the source
    d)   Enable cross-region replication for the S3 bucket to all regions

396. A company wants to store 20TB worth of scanned files. They are required to have a search application in place to search application in place to search through the scanned files.

    a)   Use a single-AZ RDS MySQL instance to store the search index for the scanned files and use an EC2 instance with a custom application to search based on the index.
    b)   Use S3 with standard redundancy to store and serve the scanned files. Use CloudSearch for the query (processing, and use Elastic Beanstalk to host the website across multiple Availability zones)
    c)   Model the environment using CloudFormation. Use an EC2 instance running Apache webserver and an open source search application, stripe multiple standard EBS volumes together to store the scanned files with a search index.
    d)   Use S3 with reduced redundancy to store and serve the scanned files. Install a commercial search (Application on EC2 instance and configure with Auto-Scaling and an Elastic Load Balancer)

397. You are an employee of an organization an work there as an AWS architect; Organization has an on-premises data center. They want to connect their on-premises infa to AWS cloud. How can this be achieved?

   a)   Use AWS VPN
   b)   Use AWS VPC Peering
   c)   Use AWS direct connect
   d)   Use Aws Express Route

398. A worry raised in your organization is that developers could potentially delete production-based EC2 resources. As a Cloud Admin, which of the below options would you choose to help alleviate this worry? Choose 2 options.

   a)   Tag the production instances with a production-identifying tag and add resource-level permissions to the developers with an explicit deny on the terminate API call to instances with the production tag.
   b)   Create a separate AWS account and add the developers to that account
   c)   Modify the IAM policy on the developers to require MFA before deleting EC2 instances, and disable MFA access to the employee.
   d)   Modify the IAM policy on the developers to require MFA before deleting EC2 instances.

399. An organization wants to observe and monitor the write and read IOPS metrics for their Amazon web services MySQL RDS instance and send real-time alerts to their Operations team. Which Amazon web services can accomplish this? Choose 2 answers

   a)   Amazon SNS
   b)   Amazon Cloudwatch
   c)   Amazon Route 53
   d)   Amazon SQS

400. You run an ad-supported photo-sharing website using S3 to server images to peoples of your site. At some point you discover out that other sites have been linking to images on your site, causing damage to your business.

Find an effective method to mitigate this? Choose the answer from the options below.

   a) Use CloudFront distribution for static content

b) Remove public read access and use signed URLs with expiry dates
c) Store photos on an EBS volume of the web server
d) Block the IPs of the offending websites in the security group

401.   An organization needs to setup a template for deploying resources to AWS. They want this to be dynamic in nature so that the template can pick up parameters and then spin up resources based on those parameters. Which of the following AWS services would be ideal for this requirement?

a) AWS CodeDeploy
b) AWS CodeBuild
c) AWS CloudFormation
d) AWS Beanstalk

402.   In an organization, their IT Security department has mandated that all data on EBS volumes created for underlying EC2 Instances needs to be encrypted. Find the best solution to achieve this?

a) AWS KMS
b) AWS Certificate Manager
c) API Gateway with STS
d) IAM Access Key

403.   An organization's business continuity department is concerned about the EBS Volumes hosted in AWS and wants to ensure that redundancy is achieved for the same. Find the best solution to achieve this in a cost-effective manner?

a)   Copy the data to a DynamoDB table for data redundancy
b)   Copy the data to S3 bucket for data redundancy
c)   Create EBS snapshots in another Availability zone for data redundancy
d)   Nothing, since by default, EBS volumes are required within their Availability zone

404.   You made a mobile application which is hosted on AWS need to access a data store in AWS. With each item measuring around 20KB in size, the latency of data access must

remain consistent despite very high application traffic. Find the best solution for Data Store for the application?

a)   AWS Redshift
b)   AWS Glacier
c)   AWS EBS Volumes
d)   AWS DynamoDB

405.   An organization is planning to design a Microservices architectured application which will be hosted in AWS. This entire architecture needs to be decoupled whenever possible. Find the best solution that can help to achieve this?

a)   AWS SQS
b)   AWS Auto Scaling
c)   AWS ELB
d)   AWS SNS

406.   You are an employee in an organization and developing a mobile application that needs to issue temporary security credentials to users. This is essential due to security concerns. Find the best solution that can help to achieve this?

a)   AWS STS
b)   AWS config
c)   AWS Trusted Advisor
d)   AWS Inspector

407.   You develop an application which is currently consist of EC2 instance sitting behind a classic ELB. The EC2 Instances are used to serve an application and are accessible through the internet. What can be done to improve this architecture in the event that the number of users accessing the application increases?

a)   Use Auto-scaling group
b)   Use the Elastic Container service
c)   Use an Application load balancer instead
d)   Add another ELB to the architecture

408. You are a developer for a gaming application which is in the design phase. Find out which of the following services can be used to ensure optimal performance and least latency for gaming users?

   a)   AWS ElastiCache
   b)   AWS ELB
   c)   AWS VPC
   d)   AWS Auto Scaling

409. The application experiences a high number of read and write requests, and you are the architect of this business intelligence application that reads data from a MySQL database hosted on an EC2 Instance.

   Which Amazon EBS volume type can meet the performance requirements of this database?
   a)   EBS provisioned IOPS SSD
   b)   EBS Cold HDD
   c)   EBS General Purpose SSD
   d)   EBS throughput optimized HDD

410. A company is planning to use AWS for their production roll out and need to implement automation for deployment like that it will automatically create a LAMP stack, download the newest PHP installable from S3 and setup the ELB. Which of the below mentioned Amazon web services meets the requirement for making an orderly deployment of the software?

   a)   AWS Elastic Beanstalk
   b)   AWS CloudFront
   c)   AWS CloudFormation
   d)   AWS DevOps

411. An organization is planning on utilizing the API Gateway service to manage APIs for developers and users. There is a need to segregate the access rights for both developers and users. Find the best solution?

   a)   Use IAM permission to control the access
   b)   Use AWS KMS service to manage the access

c)   Use AWS Access Key to manage the access

d)   Use AWS config Service to control the access

412.   A company currently have 2 development environments hosted in 2 different VPCs in an AWS account in the same region. There is now a need for resources from one VPC to access another. Find the best solution?

a)   Establish a VPC peering

b)   Establish a VPN connection

c)   Establish a Direct Connect Connection

d)   Establish Subnet Peering

413.   An organization is planning on utilizing the EMR service available in AWS for running their big data framework and wants to reduce the cost of running the EMR service. Find the best solution that helps to achieve this.

a)   Choosing Spot instances for the underlying nodes

b)   Running the EMR cluster in a dedicated VPC

c)   Choosing On-Demand instances for the underlying nodes

d)   Disable automated backups

414.   You need to provide access to users for a limited duration of time. You have an S3 bucket hosted in AWS which is used to store promotional videos you upload. How can this be achieved?

a)   Use pre-signed URLs

b)   Use IAM roles with a timestamp to limit the access

c)   Use IAM policies with a timestamp to limit the access

d)   Use versioning and enable a timestamp for each version

415.   An application presently writes a huge number of records to a DynamoDB table in one region. There is a need for a secondary application to retrieve new records written to the DynamoDB table every two hours and process the updates accordingly. Find the best ideal way to ensure that the secondary application gets the relevant changes from the DynamoDB table?

a) Use dynamoDB streams to monitor the changes in the dynamoDB table
b) Transfer records to S3 which were modified in the last two hours
c) Create another dynamoDB table with the records modified in last two hours
d) Insert a timestamp for each record and then scan the entire table for the timestamp as per the last two hours

416. Your organization has recently started using AWS services for their daily operations. As a cloud administrator, which of the following services would you recommend using to have an insight on securing the infrastructure and for cost optimization?

a) AWS Trusted Acvisor
b) AWS Inspector
c) AWS WAF
d) AWS Config

417. An IT Security depart has mandated that all traffic is flowing in and out of EC2 instances required to be observed. Which of the below services can help achieve this?

a) VPC Flow Logs
b) Trusted Advisor
c) Use CloudTrail
d) Use CloudWatch metrics

418. An organization is currently using Redshift cluster as their warehouse. As a cloud architect, you are tasked to ensure that the disaster recovery is in place. Find out which of the following options is best for addressing this issue?

a) Enable cross region snapshots for the redshift cluster
b) Create a cloudformation template to restore the cluster in another region
c) Enable cross availability zone snapshot for the redshift cluster
d) Take a copy of the underlying EBS volumes to S3 and then do cross-region replication

419. You have an AWS RDS PostgreSQL database hosted in the Landon region. You required to ensure that a backup database is in place and the data is asynchronously copied. Which of the following would help fulfill this requirement?

a)   Enable read replicas for the database
b)   Enable asynchronous replication for the database
c)   Enable manual backups for the database
d)   Enable multi AZ for the database

420.   Ahmed current log analysis application takes more than 4 hours to generate a report of the top 10 clients of your web application. He has been asked to implement a system that can report this information in real time, confirm that the report is always up to date, and handle increases in the number of requests to your web application.

Choose the option that is cost effective and can fulfill the requirements.
   a) Post your log data to an Amazon Kinesis data stream, and subscribe your log-processing application, so that is configured to process your logging data.
   b) Publish your data to CloudWatch Logs, and configure your application to Auto Scale to handle the load on demand.
   c) Publish your log data to an Amazon S3 bucket. Use AWS CloudFormation to create an Auto Scaling group to scale your post-processing application which is configured to pull down your log files stored in Amazon S3.
   d) Configure an auto scaling group to increase the size of your Amazon EMR cluster

421.   Your organization requires to automate the deployment of new EC2 Instances. There is a need to have pre-baked Images so that the deployment of instances can be done in a faster manner. Which of the following options can help achieve this?

   a) Create an Amazon machine image
   b) Create an EC2 image
   c) Create an Opsworks image
   d) Create an elastic beanstalk image

422.   There is a need to load a lot of information from your on-premises network on to AWS Redshift. Find the best options that can be used for this data transfer?

Choose any 2 answers from the options given below.
   a) Direct Connect
   b) Snowball

c) Data pipeline

d) AWS VPN

423. Having created a Redshift cluster in AWS, you are trying to use SQL Client tools from an EC2 Instance, but are not able to connect to the Redshift Cluster. What must you do to ensure that you can connect to the Redshift Cluster from the EC2 Instance?

a) Modify the VPC security group

b) Use the AWS CLI instead of the redshift client tools

c) Modify the NACL on the subnet

d) Install redshift client tools on the EC2 instance first

424. You currently an employee of an organization that is specialized in baggage management. GPS devices installed on all the baggages, deliver the coordinates of the unit every 10 seconds. You need to process these coordinates in real-time from multiple sources. Which tool should you use to process the data?

a)   Amazon kinesis

b)   AWS Data Pipeline

c)   Amazon SQS

d)   Amazon EMR

425. Hammad is planning on hosting a web and database application in an AWS VPC. The database must only be accessible by the web server.

Find the best option that fulfills this requirement?

a)   Security groups

b)   Route table

c)   AWS RDS parameter group

d)   Network Access control list

426. An organization needs block-level storage which should be able to store 800GB of data. Also, coding of the data is required. Find the best option for this case?

a)   AWS ESB volumes

b)   AWS EFS

c)   AWS Glacier

d)   AWS S3

427.   Hammad has an application that needs storage for an EC2 Instance for storing infrequently accessed data. Which of the following is a cost-effective, ideal storage option here?

a)   EBS cold HDD
b)   EBS Throughput Optimized
c)   EBS SSD
d)   EBS IOPS

428.   You are a cloud administrator of your organization, you notice that one of the EC2 instances is restarting again and again. There is a requirement to troubleshooting and analyze the system logs. What can be used in AWS to store and analyze the log files from the EC2 Instance? Select any one answer from the options below.

a)   AWS CloudWatch Logs
b)   AWS CloudTrail
c)   AWS S3
d)   AWS SQS

429.   An organization migrated their production environment into AWS VPC 7 months ago. As a cloud architect, you need to revise the infrastructure and ensure that it is profitable in the long term. There are more than 50 EC2 instances that are up and running all the time to support the business operation. Find the best solution to lower the cost?

a)   Reserved instances
b)   On-demand instances
c)   Spot Instances
d)   Regular instances

430.   You are Solutions architect, it is your job to design a highly accessible and fault tolerant infrastructure. Your organization is utilizing Amazon S3 to store huge amounts of file data. What steps would you take to confirm that if an AZ were misplaced because of natural disaster, your files would still be in place and accessible?

a)   Amazon S3 is highly available and fault tolerant by design and requires no additional configuration

b)   Copy the S3 bucket to an EBS optimized backed EC2 instance

c)   Enable cross-region replication for the S3 bucket

d)   Enable AWS storage gateway using gateway stored setup

431.   An organization may rarely need to retrieve these logs for audit purposes and present them upon request within 7 days. The logs are 10TB in size. Find the best cost-effective solution.

a) Amazon Glacier

b) AWS CloudFront

c) EBS backed storage connected to EC2

d) S3 Reduced redundancy storage

432.   An organization is building service using Amazon EC2 as a worker instance that will process uploaded audio files and generate a text file. Their employee must store both of these files in the same durable storage until the text file is retrieved. Their employee does not know what the storage capacity requirements are.

Find storage that covers both cost-efficient and scalable?

a)   Single Amazon S3 bucket

b)   Multiple instance store

c)   Single Amazon glacier vault

d)   Multiple Amazon EBS volume with snapshots

433.   A company has configured an Auto-scaling group for which the minimum running instance is 2, and the maximum running instance is 10. For the past 35 minutes, all 5 instances have been running on 100 (CPU) Utilization. Still, the Auto Scaling group has not added any more instances to the group.

Find the cause for this? Select any 2

a)   The auto-scaling groups scale up policy has not yet been reached

b)   You already have 20 on demand instances running

c)   The auto-scaling groups MAX size is set at 5

d)   The auto-scaling groups scale down policy is too high

434. An organization is using CloudFront to distribute its media content to multiple regions. The content is frequently accessed by the client. As a cloud architect, Find best solution to improve the performance of the system.

    a) Increasing the cache expiration time
    b) Use a faster internet connection
    c) Crate an Invalidation for all you object, and re-cache them
    d) Change the origin location from an S3 bucket to an ELB

435. An employee has been instructed by his boss to devise a disaster recovery model for the resources in their AWS account. The key requirement while devising the solution is to guarantee that the cost is at a minimum. Find the best solution in this case.

    a) Backup and restore
    b) Multi site
    c) Warm standby
    d) Pilot light

436. An application consists of the following architecture
    • The EC2 instance is launched via an auto-scaling group
    • EC2 instance is in multiple AZ's behind an ELB
    • There is a NAT instance used so that instance can download updates from the internet Due to the high bandwidth being consumed by the NAT instance, it has been decided to use a NAT Gateway. How should this be implemented?

Select any one
    a) Migrate the NAT instance to NAT gateway and host the NAT gateway in the public subnet
    b) Convert the NAT instance to a NAT gateway
    c) Host the NAT instance in the private subnet
    d) Use NAT instance along with the NAT gateway

437. A company has an application hosted in AWS. This application consists of EC2 Instances that sit behind an ELB with EC2 Instances. The following are requirements from an administrative perspective:
    • Ensure that notification is sent when the latency goes beyond 10 sec

- Must be able to collect and analyze logs with regard to ELB's performance

Find out which of the following can be used to achieve requirements?
Select any two:
   a) Enable the logs on the ELB and then investigate the logs whenever there is an issue
   b) Use cloudwatch for monitoring
   c) Enable cloud watch logs and then investigate the logs whenever there is an issue
   d) Use cloudtrail to monitor whatever metrics need to be monitored

438. An organization would like to leverage the AWS storage option and integrate it with the current on-premises infrastructure. Besides, due to requirements, low latency access to all the data is necessary.

Find the best solution that suited for this scenario?
   a) Configure storage gateway stored volume
   b) Configure Amazon glacier
   c) Configure storage gateway-cached volume
   d) Configure the simple storage service

439. An IT organization has a set of EC2 Instances hosted in a VPC. They are hosted in a private subnet. These instances now required to access resources stored in an S3 bucket. The traffic should not traverse the internet. The addition of which of the following would help fulfill this requirement?

   a) VPC Endpoint
   b) Nat Gateway
   c) Nat Instance
   d) Internet gateway

440. Ahmed wants to host a set of web servers and database servers in an AWS VPC. Find out which of the following is a best practice in designing a multi-tier infrastructure?

   a)   Use a public subnet for the web tier and a private subnet for the database layer
   b)   Use a public subnet for the web tier and a public subnet for the database layer
   c)   Use a private subnet for the web tier and a private subnet for the database layer
   d)   Use a private subnet for the web tier and a private subnet for the database layer

441. An IT organization would like to secure their resources in their AWS Account. Which of the following options is able to secure data at rest and in transit in AWS?

Choose any 3 answers from the options given below.

a) Use server-side Encryption for S3
b) Use SSL/HTTPS when using the elastic load balancer
c) Encrypt all EBS volume attached to EC2 Instances
d) Use IOPS volume when working with EBS volumes on EC2 Instances

442. An organization currently has a set of EC2 Instances running a web application which sits behind an Elastic Load Balancer. The organization also have an Amazon RDS instance which is accessible from the web application. The organization has been asked to ensure that this architecture is self-healing in nature and cost-effective.

Which of the following would fulfill this requirement?

Select any two:

a) Use CloudWatch metrics to check the utilization of the web layer. Use Auto Scaling Group to scale the web instances accordingly based on the CloudWatch metrics.
b) Utilize the Multi AZ feature for the Amazon RDS layer
c) Use CloudWatch metrics to check the utilization of the databases servers. Use Auto Scaling Group to scale the database instances accordingly based on the CloudWatch metrics.
d) Utilize the read replica feature for the Amazon RDS layer.

443. Your organization has a set of EC2 Instances that access data objects stored in an S3 bucket. Your IT Security department is concerned about the security of this architecture and wants you to implement the following:

• Prevent accidental deletion of an object
• Ensure that the EC2 Instance securely accessed the data object stored in the S3 bucket

Find the best solution to fulfill the requirements

Select any 2

a) Use an S3 bucket policy that ensures that MFA Delete is set on the objects in the bucket.

b) Create an IAM Role and ensure the EC2 Instances use the IAM Role to access the data in the bucket.

c) Create an IAM user and ensure the EC2 Instances use the IAM user credentials to access the data in the bucket.

d) Use S3 Cross-Region Replication to replicate the objects so that the integrity of data is maintained.

444. You are an employee of an organization, and you have a requirement to get a snapshot of the current configuration of resources in your AWS Account. Find bets service for this purpose:

a) AWS Config
b) AWS IAM
c) AWS trusted advisor
d) AWS codedeploy

445. Your Organization is hosting an application in AWS.
   • The application is read intensive and consists of a set of web servers and AWS RDS.
   • It has been noticed that the response time of the application decreases due to the load on the AWS RDS instance.

Find out which of the following measures can be taken to scale the data tier?
Select any two:

a) Create Amazon DB Read Replicas. Configure the application layer to query the Read Replicas for query needs.

b) Use elasticache in front of your Amazon RDS DB to cache common queries

c) Use SQS to cache the database Queries

d) Use Auto Scaling to scale out and scale in the database tier

446. Your organization is now planning on hosting a set of EC2 Instances in AWS.
   • The Instances would be divided into subnets, one for the web tier and the other for the database tier.
   • The web tier would be exposed to the Internet via the Internet gateway.

As an architect, which of the following would be needed to guarantee that traffic can flow between the Instances in each subnet.

a) Ensure that the security groups have the required rules defined to allow traffic

b) Ensure that the route tables have the desired routing between the subnets

c) Ensure that all subnet is defined as public subnets

d) Ensure that all subnets are defined as public subnets

447. A group of people has developed an application, and now they required to deploy that application onto an EC2 Instance. This application interacts with a DynamoDB table. Find the correct and MOST SECURE way.

a) Create a role which has the necessary and can be assumed by the EC2 instance.

b) Use the API credentials from a bastion host. Make the application on the EC2 Instance send requests via the bastion host.

c) Use the API credentials from a NAT Instance. Make the application on the EC2 Instance send requests via the NAT Instance

d) Use the API credentials from an EC2 instance. Ensure the environment variables are updated with the API access keys.

448. Ahmed is planning to utilize the MySQL RDS in AWS. He has a requirement to ensure that you are available to recover from a database crash. As an architect which of the following can he use to recover from a database crash.

Select any two

a) Use the multi AZ feature for the database

b) Ensure that automated backups are enabled for the RDS

c) Ensure that the database is encrypted at rest

d) Ensure that you define multiple endpoints for the database

449. Your xyz organization is big on building container-based applications. Currently, they use Kubernete. They want to move to AWS and preferably not have to manage the infrastructure for the underlying orchestration service.

Find the best solution for this case?

a) AWS ECS

b) AWS BynamoDB

c) AWS EC2 with Kubernetes installed

d) AWS Elastic Beanstalk

450. An organization is looking at reducing the amount of time it takes to build servers, which are deployed as EC2 Instances. These Instances always have the similar type of software installed as per the security standards. As an architect what would you recommend in decreasing the server build time?

    a) Create a base AMI
    b) Create a base profile
    c) Create the same master copy of the EBS volume
    d) Look at creating a snapshot of EBS volume

451. Ahmed is an architect he has been told to construct the deployment design for an application. He wants to ensure that the application is fault tolerant. When using the following Amazon web services, which should be implemented in multiple Availability Zones for high availability solutions?

Select any two option
    a) Amazon elastic load balancing
    b) Amazon elastic compute cloud (EC2)
    c) Amazon DynamoDB
    d) Amazon Simple Storage Services (S3)

452. Hamza is designing the following application in Amazon web services.
    • Users will use the application to upload videos and images.
    • The files will then be picked up by a worker process for further processing.

Which of the below services should be used in the design of the application.

Select any two
    a) AWS SQS for distributed processing of messages by the worker process
    b) AWS simple storage service for storing the videos and images
    c) AWS glacier for storing the videos and images
    d) AWS SNS for distributed processing of the message by the worker process

453. Ahmed's development group has created a web application that needs to be tested on VPC. You want to advise the IT admin group on how they should implement the VPC to ensure the application can be accessed from the Internet.

Find the following components that would be part of the design.

Select any 3

a) All instances launched with a public IP
b) Route table entry added for the internet gateway
c) An internet gateway attached to the VPC
d) A NAT gateway attached to the VPC

454. An organization is planning on deploying an application which contains web and database tier. The database tier should not be accessible from the Internet.

How would you design the networking part of the application?
Select any two

a) A private subnet for the database tier
b) A public subnet for the database tier
c) A private subnet for the database tier
d) A public subnet for the web tier

455. Ammar is creating a number of EBS Volumes for the EC2 Instances hosted in his organization's Amazon web services account. The organization has asked him to ensure that the EBS volumes are available even in the event of a disaster. How would he accomplish this?

Select any two

a) Creating snapshot of the EBS volumes
b) Ensure the snapshots are made available in another region
c) Ensure the snapshots are made available in another region
d) Configure Amazon Storage Gateway with EBS volumes as the data source and store the backups on-premise through the storage gateway

456. Arfa is planning to host a static website on an EC2 Instance. She wants to ensure that the environment is highly available and scalable to meet demand. Which of the below aspects can be utilized to create a highly available environment.

Select any three

a) Multiple availability zones
b) Elastic load balancer
c) An auto scaling group to recover from EC2 instance failures
d) An SQS queue

457. Amaar's organizations are hosting a set of crucial documents in an S3 bucket. There is a requirement to ensure that documents are also available in the event of a disaster.

How can he achieve this?
   a) Enable cross-region replication for the underlying bucket
   b) Enable multi AZ Replication for the underlying bucket
   c) Use the AWS CLI to copy the object from the S3 bucket to an EBS volume
   d) Use the AWS CLI to copy the object from the S3 bucket to another availability zone

458. You currently work for an organization that has a set of EC2 Instances. There is an internal need to create another instance in another availability zone. One of the EBS volumes from the current instance needs to be moved from one of the older instances to the new instance. How can this be achieved?

   a)   Create a snapshot of the volume and then create a volume from the snapshot in the other AZ
   b)   Create a new volume in the AZ and do a disk copy of contents from one volume to another
   c)   Create a new volume in the other AZ and specify the current volume as the source
   d)   Detach the volume and attach to an EC2 instance in another AZ

459. Yousuf has a requirement to host a web-based application. He needs to enable high availability for the application, so he creates an Elastic Load Balancer and places the EC2 Instances behind the Elastic Load Balancer. He wants to ensure that clients only access the application via the DNS name of the load balancer. How would you design the network part of the application?

Select any two
   a)   Create 2 private subnets for the backend instances
   b)   Create 2 public subnet for the Elastic load balancer
   c)   Create 2 private subnet for the Elastic load balancer
   d)   Create 2 public subnet for the backend instances

460. Ammar's organization has a large set of resources hosted on Amazon web services. His organization wants to keep a check on the Active Volumes, Active snapshots and Elastic IP addresses you use so that he does not go beyond the service limit.

Which of the below services can help in this regard?

a) AWS Trusted Advisor
b) AWS EC2
c) AWS SNS
d) AWS Cloudwatch

461. You are working for an organization act as an architect. The organization normally creates the same set of resources for their costumer. They need some way of building templates, which can then be used to deploy the resources to the Amazon web services accounts for the various costumer.

Which of the following service can help fulfill this requirement?

a) AWS Cloudformation
b) AWS SQS
c) AWS SNS
d) AWS Elastic Beanstalk

462. You are working for an organization act as an architect. An application is going to be installed on a set of EC2 instances in a VPC. You need to guarantee that IT administrators can securely administer the instances in the VPC.

How can you accomplish this?

a) Create a bastion host in the public subnet. Make IT admin staff use this as a jump server to the backend instances.
b) Create a bastion host in the private subnet. Make IT admin staff use this as a jump server to the backend instances.
c) Create a NAT instance in a public subnet, ensure SSH access is provided to the NAT instance. Access the Instances via the NAT instance.
d) Create a NAT gateway, ensure SSH access is provided to the NAT gateway. Access the Instances via the NAT gateway.

463. You are working for an organization act as an architect. An application is going to be deployed on a set of EC2 instances in a VPC. The Instances will be hosting a web application. You want to design the security group to confirm that users have the ability

to connect from the Internet via HTTPS. Find out which of the following needs to be configured for the security group.

a) Allow Inbound access on port 433 for 0.0.0.0/0
b) Allow Outbound access on port 433 for 0.0.0.0/0
c) Allow Inbound access on port 80 for 0.0.0.0/0
d) Allow Outbound access on port 80 for 0.0.0.0/0

464. An organization runs an automobile reselling organization that has an online store on Amazon web services. The application sits behind an Auto Scaling group and needs new instances of the Auto Scaling group to identify their private and public IP addresses. As an employee, you need to inform the development team on how they can achieve this. Find the best solution

a) Using a Curl or Get Command to get the latest meta-data from http://169.254.169.254/latest/meta-data/
b) Using a Curl or Get Command to get the latest user-data from http://169.254.169.254/latest/user-data/
c) By using a cloud watch metric
d) By using ipconfig for windows of ifconfig for Linux

465. You are an employee in an organization, and you have been designing a CloudFormation template that makes one elastic load balancer fronting two EC2 instances. Which section of the template should you edit so that the DNS of the load balancer is returned upon creation of the stack?

a) Outputs
b) Mappings
c) Parameters
d) Resources

466. An organization has a set of VPC's defined in AWS. They want to connect this to their on-premises network. They need to confirm that all data is encrypted in transit. Find out which of the following would you use to connect the VPC's to the on-premises networks?

a) VPN connection
b) VPC peering
c) AWS Direct Connect
d) Placement Groups

467.   An organization needs to host a selection of MongoDB instances. They are expecting a great load and required to have as low latency as possible. As an architect, you want to guarantee that the right storage is used to host the MongoDB database. Which of the following would you incorporate as the underlying storage layer?

a) Provisioned IOPS
b) Cold HDD
c) Throughput Optimized HDD
d) General Purpose SSD

468.   Ahmad's organization has a set of EC2 Instances hosted on the AWS Cloud. As an architect, he has been told to ensure that if the status of any of instances is related to a failure, then the instances are automatically restarted. Find a most effective way to solve this.

a) Create a cloudwatch alarm that stops and start the instance based off of status check alarm
b) Implement a third-party monitoring tool
c) Write a script that periodically shut down and starts instances based on certain stats
d) Write a script that queries the EC2 API for each instance status check

469.   An organization is planning on migrating their infrastructure to Amazon web services. For the data stores, the organization doesn't need to manage the underlying infrastructure. Find out which of the following would be ideal for this scenario?

Select any two from the following
a) AWS DynamoDB
b) AWS S3
c) AWS EBS Volumes
d) AWS EC2

470.   Ammar's organization has a set of resources defined in Amazon web services. These resources comprise of applications hosted on EC2 Instances. Data is stored on EBS volumes and S3. The organization mandates that all data should be encoded at rest. How can you achieve this?

Select any 2 from the following
   a) Enable S3 Server-side Encryption
   b) Enable EBS Encryption
   c) Enable SSL with the underlying EBS volume
   d) Make sure that data is transmitted from S3 via HTTPS

471.   Hammad's organization has a web application hosted in Amazon web services that make usage of an Application Load Balancer. He wants to confirm that the web application is protected from web-based attacks such as cross-site scripting etc.

Which of the following implementation steps can help protect web applications from common security threats from the outside world?
   a) Use the WAF service in front of the web application
   b) Place a NAT instance in front of the web application to protect against attacks
   c) Place the wen application in front of a CDN service instead
   d) Place a NAT gateway in front of the web application to protect against attacks

472.   Asad's boss asks him to create a decoupled application whose process includes dependencies on EC2 instances and servers located in your organization's on-premises data center.

Find out which of the following would you include in the architecture?
   a) An SQS queue as the messaging component between the instances and servers
   b) Route 53 resource records to route requests based on failure
   c) An elastic load balancer records to route request based on failure
   d) An SNS topic as the messaging component between the instances and servers

473.   A client required corporate IT governance and cost oversight of all Amazon web services resources spent by its divisions. Each division has their own Amazon web services account, and there is a requirement to confirm that the security policies are kept in place at the Account Level. How can you achieve this?

Select any two
   a) User service control policies

b) Use AWS organization

c) Club all division under a single account instead

d) Use IAM policies to segregate access

474. Hamza's organization has a set of VPC's. There is now a requirement to establish communication across the Instances in the VPC's. His boss has asked him to implement the VPC peering connection. Which of the following considerations would you keep in mind for VPC peering?

Select any two from the following:

a) Ensuring that no on-premises communication is required via transitive routing

b) Ensuring that the VPC's do not have overlapping CIDR blocks

c) Ensuring that the VPC's are created in the same region

d) Ensuring that the VPC's are created in the same region

475. Ammar has been instructed to establish a successful site-to-site VPN connection from his on-premises network to the VPC. As an architect, which of the following pre-requisites should he ensure are in place for establishing the site-to-site VPN connection. Select any two from the following:

a) A virtual private gateway attached to the VPC

b) A public IP address on the customer gateway for the on-premises network

c) An elastic IP address to the virtual private gateway

d) The main route table to route traffic through a NAT instance

476. Hammad's organization wants to enable encryption of services such as EBS and S3 volumes so that the data it maintains is encrypted at rest. They need to have complete control over the keys and the entire lifecycle around the keys.

How can you accomplish this?

a) Use the HSM module

b) Enable EBS Encryption with the default KMS keys

c) Enable S3 server-side Encryption

d) Use the KMS service

477. An organization wants to implement a data store in Amazon web services. The data store needs to have the following requirements
    - Scale based on demand
    - Ability to store JSON objects efficiently
    - Complete managed by AWS

Which of the following would an employee use as the data store
   a) AWS DynamoDB
   b) AWS Redshift
   c) AWS Glacier
   d) AWS Aurora

478. An organization has setup some EC2 Instances in a VPC with the default Security group and NACL settings. They need to confirm that IT admin staff can connect to the EC2 Instance via SSH. As an architect what would you ask the IT admin team to do to ensure that they can connect to the EC2 Instance from the Internet?

Select any two from the following:
   a) Ensure to modify the security group
   b) Ensure that the instance has a public or elastic IP
   c) Ensure to modify the NACL rules
   d) Ensure that the instance has a private IP

479. Hanif's organization has a set of EBS volumes and a set of adjoining EBS snapshots. They need to minimize the costs for the underlying EBS snap shots.

Which of the following approaches provides the lowest cost for Amazon Elastic Block Store snapshots while giving you the ability to fully restore data?

   a) Maintain a single snapshot the latest snapshot is both incremental and complete
   b) Maintain the most current snapshot, archive the original and incremental to Amazon Glacier.
   c) Maintain two snapshots: the original snapshot and the latest incremental snapshot.
   d) Maintain a volume snapshot; subsequent snapshots will overwrite one another.

480. Khawar is using an m1. Small EC2 Instance with one 300GB EBS General purpose SSD volume to host a relational database. He determined that write throughput to the database wants to be increased.

Find out which of the following approaches can help achieve this?

Select any two from the following:

a) Consider using provisioned IOPS Volumes

b) Use a large EC2 instance

c) Put the database behind an elastic load balancer

d) Enable multi AZ feature for the database

481. An organization has a set of AWS RDS Instances. Your management has asked you to deactivate Automated backups to save on cost. When you deactivate automated backups for AWS RDS.

What are you compromising on?

a) You are disabling the point in time recovery

b) Nothing you are actually saving on AWS

c) You cannot disable automated backups in RDS

d) Nothing really you can still take manual backups

482. An organization is planning to install a web-based application. They want to confirm that users across the world have the ability to view the pages from the website with the least amount of latency.

How can you accomplish this?

a) Place a CloudFront distribution in front of the web application

b) Use rout 53 with latency based routing

c) Place an elastic cache in front of the web application

d) Place an elastic load balancer in front of the web application

483. A client is hosting their organization website on a cluster of web servers that are behind a public-facing load balancer. The client also uses Amazon Route 53 to manage their public DNS.

How should Route 53 be configured to ensure the custom domain is made to point to the load balancer?

Select any 2 from the following

a) Create an alias for CNAME record to the load balancer DNS name

b) Ensure that a hosted zone is in place

c) Create a CNAME record pointing to the load balancer DNS name

d) Create an A record pointing to the IP address of the load balancer

484. A client is hosting their organization website on a cluster of web servers that are behind a public-facing load balancer. The web application interfaces with an AWS RDS database. It has been noticed that a set of similar types of queries is causing a performance bottleneck at the database layer.

Which of the following architecture additions can help alleviate this issue?"
   a) Deploy elasticache in front of the database server
   b) Deploy elasticache in front of the web server
   c) Enable multi AZ for the database
   d) Deploy Elastic load balancer in front of the web servers

485. A client is hosting their organization website on a cluster of web servers that are behind a public-facing load balancer. The web application interfaces with an AWS RDS database. The management has specified that the database is available in case of a hardware failure on the primary database. The secondary needs to be made available in the least amount of time.

Which of the following would you opt for?
   a) Enable multi AZ failover
   b) Made a snapshot of the database
   c) Created a read replica
   d) Increase the database instance size

486. Your organization wants on launching a set of EC2 Instances for hosting their production-based web application. As an architect, you have to instruct the operations department on which service they can use for the monitoring purposes.

Which of the following would you recommend?
   a) AWS cloudwatch
   b) AWS cloudtrail
   c) AWS SQS
   d) AWS SNS

487. An organization is planning on storing their files from their on-premises location onto the Simple Storage service. After a period of 2.5 months, they need to archive the files, since they would be rarely used.

Find out which of the following would be the right way to service this requirement?

a) Store the data on S3 and then use Lifecycle policies to transfer the data to Amazon Glacier
b) Use an EC2 instance with EBS volumes. After a period of 2.5 months, keep on taking snapshots of the data.
c) Use an EC2 instance with EBS volumes. After a period of 2.5 months, keep on taking copies of the volume using Cold HDD volume type.
d) Store the data on Amazon Glacier and then use Lifecycle policies to transfer the data to Amazon S3

488.	An organization has a workflow that sends video files from their on-premises system to Amazon web services for transcoding. They utilize EC2 worker instances that pull transcoding jobs from SQS. As an architect, you want to design how the SQS service would be used in this architecture.

Find out which of the following is the ideal way in which the SQS service should be used?
a) SQS should be used to facilitate horizontal scaling of encoding tasks
b) SQS should be used to check the health of the worker instances
c) SQS should be used to synchronously manage the transcoding output
d) SQS should be used to guarantee the order of the message

489.	Ahmed is an architect in his organization. His IT admin staff wants access to newly created EC2 Instances for administrative purposes. Which of the following needs to be done to confirm that the IT admin staff can successfully connect via port 22 on to the EC2 Instances

a) Adjust the instance's security group to permit ingress traffic over port 22 from your IP
b) Modify the instance security group to allow ingress over port 22 from your IP
c) Configure the IAM role to permit changes to security group settings
d) Adjust security group to permit egress traffic over TCP port 443 from your IP

490.	Ammar's organization is running an image sharing website. Currently, all the images are stored in S3. At some point the organization finds out that other sites have been linking to the images on his site, causing loss to your business. He wants to implement a solution for the organization to mitigate this issue.

Find the best solution for this issue

a) Remove public read access and use signed URLs with expiry dates
b) Store images on an EBS volume of the web server
c) Block the IPs of the offending websites in the security group
d) Use cloud front distribution for static content

491. Hanif has been hired as a consultant for an organization to implement their CI/CD processes. They currently use an on-premises deployment of Chef for their configuration management on servers. Hanif wants to advise them on what they can use on Amazon web services to leverage their existing capabilities.

Find the best recommendation for this case
a) AWS OpsWorks
b) AWS CloudFormation
c) AWS Elastic Beanstalk
d) Amazon SWS

492. Hammad has been hired as a consultant for an organization to implement their CI/CD processes. They have a keen eye to implement the deployment of their infrastructure as code. Hammad wants to advise them on what they can use on Amazon web services to fulfill this requirement.

Find the best recommendation for this case
a) AWS cloudformation
b) AWS OpsWorks
c) AWS Elastic Beanstalk
d) Amazon SWS

493. Yousuf work as an architect for an organization. There is a need for an application to be deployed on a set of EC2 Instances. These would be part of a compute cluster that requires low inter-node latency.

Find the best solution for this case
a) Cluster placement group
b) EC2 dedicated instances
c) AWS direct connect
d) Multiple availability zones

494.   Hammad's organization stores a huge set of files in Amazon S3. They want to ensure that if any new files are added to an S3 bucket, an event notification would be sent to the IT admin staff.

Find out which of the following could be used to fulfill this requirement?

Select any 2 from the following

a) Add an event notification to the S3 bucket
b) Create an SNS topic
c) Add an event notification to the S3 object
d) Create an SQS queue

495.   Ammar's organization is planning on migrating their code from their on-premises infrastructure onto Amazon web services. They want to ensure to limit the amount of maintenance that would be required for the underlying infrastructure.

Which of the following would they choose for hosting the code base?

a) AWS Lambda
b) AWS SQS
c) AWS ECS
d) AWS EC2

496.   An organization has an Amazon web services account that contains 3 VPCs (Dev, Test, and Prod) in the same region. There is a requirement to ensure that instances in the Development and Test VPC can access resources in the Production VPC for a limited amount of time.

Which of the following would be the ideal way to get this in place?

a)   Create a separate VPC peering connection from Development to Production and from Test to the Production VPC
b)   Create an AWS Direct Connect connection between the Development, Test VPC to the Production VPC
c)   Create a VPC peering connection between the Development to the Production VPC and from Development to the Test VPC.
d)   Create a VPN connection between the Development, Test VPC to the Production VPC

497. Anwar is designing the application architecture for an organization. The architecture is going to comprise of a web tier that will be hosted on EC2 Instances placed behind an Elastic Load Balancer.

   Find out which of the following would be considered important when considering what should the specification for the components of the application architecture?
   a)   Determining the minimum memory requirements for an application
   b)   Determine the required I/O operations
   c)   Determining the peak expected usage for a client's application
   d)   Determining where the client intends to serve most of the traffic

498. Ammar's organization has a requirement to host an application in Amazon web services that need access to a NoSQL database. But there are no human resources available who can take care of the database infrastructure, and also the database should have the capability to scale automatically based on demand and also have high availability. Find out which of the following databases would you use for this purpose?

   a)   DynamoDB
   b)   Amazon Aurora
   c)   Amazon RDS
   d)   Elasticmap Reduce

499. Anwar's organization is planning on moving to the Amazon web services Cloud. There is a strict compliance policy that mandates that data should be encrypted at rest. As an Amazon web services Solution architect, Anwar has been tasked to put the organization data on the cloud and also ensure that all compliance requirements have been met. Which of the below needs to be part of the implementation plan to ensure compliance with the security requirements.

   Select any 2 from the following
   a)   Ensure that server-side encryption is enabled for an S3 bucket
   b)   Ensure that all EBS volume is encrypted
   c)   Ensure that the EC2 security rules only allow HTTPS traffic
   d)   Ensure that the SSL is enabled for all load balancers

500. Khawar's organization is planning on moving to the AWS Cloud. One of the applications will be launched on a set of EC2 Instances. He wants to confirm that the architecture is fault tolerant and highly available.

Which of the following would be considered during the design process.

Select any 2 from the following

a)   Use a load balancer in front of the EC2 instances
b)   Ensure that the EC2 instances are spread across multiple availability zones
c)   Ensure that the EC2 instances are spread across a single availability zone for better maintenance
d)   Enable multi AZ for the databases

501.   An organization needs to implement a hybrid architecture where it required to connect VPC's in its account to its on-premises architecture. There is a need, which states that all traffic wants to be encoded between the on-premises data centers and the AWS VPC's. Find out which of the following would you recommend to fulfill this requirement?

a) AWS VPN
b) AWS Direct Link
c) AWS VPC peering
d) AWS Direct Connect

502.   Fahad's organization presently has a set of EC2 Instances. His supervisor has advised that as part of the business continuity requirement that EC2 Instances should be available in another region in case the primary region goes down. He wants to confirm that Instances in the secondary region come up in the shortest possible period. Which of the following technique would you implement for this requirement?

a) Create an AMI and copy it to another region
b) Create a new instance in the new region and then install the required software's
c) Create an EBS snapshot and then copy it to another region
d) Make a new instance in the new region and then install the required software's

503.   Anwar is a solutions architect, it is your job to design for high availability and fault tolerance. The organization is using Amazon S3 to store large amounts of file data. Anwar wants to confirm that the files are available in case of a disaster.

Find the best solution to achieve this:

a) Enable CRR for the bucket

b) Enable versioning for the bucket

c) Copy the S3 bucket to an EBS optimized EC2 instance

d) Amazon S3 is extremely available and fault tolerant by design and requires no additional configuration

504.   Khawar's organization currently has a set of virtual servers that want to be migrated to the Amazon web services Cloud. These Instances are normally 75% utilized and used throughout most of the year. As a solutions architect which of the following Instance pricing model would he suggest?

a) Reserved instances

b) Spot Instances

c) Regular instances

d) On-demand instance

505.   Hammad's organization presently has a set of EC2 Instances hosted on the Amazon web services Cloud. There is a need to ensure the restart of instances if a cloudwatch metric goes beyond a certain threshold. As a solutions architect, how would he ask the IT admin staff to implement this?

a) Create a cloudwatch matric which looks at the desired metric and then restarts the server based on the threshold

b) Look at the cloudtrail logs for events and then restart the instance based on the events

c) Use the AWS config utility on the EC2 instance to check for metrics and restart the server

d) Create a CLI script that restarts the server at certain intervals

506.   You have a read-intensive application hosted in Amazon web services. The application is presently using the MySQL RDS feature in Amazon web services. The cloudwatch metrics are showing high read throughput on the database and is causing performance issues on the database. Find out Which of the following can be used to reduce the read throughput on the MySQL database?

a) Enable read replica's and offload the reads to the replica's

b) Use SQS to queue up the reads

c) Enable the multi AZ on the MySQL RDS

d) Use cold storage volume for the MySQL RDS

507. An organization is planning to move an application, which is currently hosted, on their on-premises environment onto Amazon web services. The application currently connects to a JSON based data store. They want to choose the right replacement in Amazon web services. They also want to confirm that they avoid the task of maintaining the underlying infrastructure for the database. Which of the following should they select as the underlying data store?

a) AWS DynamoDB

b) AWS RDS

c) AWS Elastic Map Reduce

d) AWS Redshift

508. Khawar's organization has started hosting their databases on the Amazon web services Cloud. As an architect, they have requested Khawar to advise the IT admin staff on what they should use to monitor the underlying databases. Notifications should be sent to IT admin staff if any issues are detected. Which Amazon web services can accomplish this requirement?

Select any two from the following

a) Amazon SNS

b) Amazon CloudWatch

c) Amazon SQS

d) Amazon Route 53

509. Khawar's organization has started hosting their data store on Amazon web services by utilizing the Simple Storage service. They are storing files, which are downloaded by users on a frequent basis. After a duration of 2 months, the files need to transferred to archive storage since they are not used beyond this point. Find out Which of the following could be used to effectively manage this requirement?

a) Use lifecycle policies to transfer the files onto glacier after a period of 2 months

b) Transfer the files via scripts from S3 to glacier after a period of 2 months

c) Create a snapshot of the files in S3 after a period of 2 months

d) Use lifecycle policies to transfer the files onto cold HDD after a period of 2 months

510. Yousuf's organization is planning on setting up a VPC with private and public subnets and then hosting EC2 Instances in the subnet. It has to be confirmed that instances in the private subnet can download updates from the internet.

Which of the following needs to be part of the architecture for this requirement?
   a) NAT Gateway
   b) WAF
   c) Direct Connect
   d) VPN

Answers

1. **B** (Create NAT gateways on both VPCs and configure routes in respective route tables with NAT gateways)

Explanation:
See AWS documentation for "Using a NAT gateway with VPC Endpoints...."

https://docs.aws.amazon.com/AmazonVPC/latest/UserGuide/vpc-nat-gateway.html#nat-gateway-basics

2. **B** (10.10.3.0/24 subnet's ACL does not have an inbound Allow rule set for all traffic)

   C (RDS security group is not correctly configured with 10.10.1.0/24 instead of 10.10.2.0/24)

Explanation:

Option B is a possible answer because security group is configured with public subnet IP range instead of private subnet 1 IP range and EC2 is in private subnet 1, so EC2 will be unable to communicate with RDS in private subnet 2.

For options C, "The default network ACL is configured to allow all traffic to flow in and out of the subnet to which it is associated. Each network ACL also includes a rule whose rule number is an asterisk (*), this rule can't be modified or removed. This asterisk rule ensures that if a packet doesn't match any of the other numbered rules, it is denied.

3. **C** (Both the subnets are associated with the main route table, no subnet is explicitly attached with new route table that has the IGW route.)

Explanation:

Whenever a subnet is created, it is associated with the main route table. If different routes are required for main and non-main route tables, you need to explicitly associate the subnet to the new, non-main route table.

4. **B** (S3 bucket is in a different region than the VPC)

Explanation:

VPC Endpoints do not support cross-region S3 requests. If the S3 bucket is in other region than the VPC, the VPC Endpoint does not take effect. In this situation, requests will go to NAT gateway as the route table has a route to it.

5. C (AWS IAM role/user does not have access to new S3 bucket)

   D (VPV Endpoint contains a policy, currently restricted to many S3 buckets and does not contain the new one)

Explanation:

VPC Endpoint has a default policy that allows all actions on all S3 buckets. We can restrict access to certain S3 buckets and certain actions on this policy. In such cases, for accessing any new buckets, VPC Endpoint policy needs to be modified accordingly.

AWS IAM role/user which is used to access S3 bucket need to have access granted via IAM policy.

6. B (Security group's outbound rules for EC2 instance are restricted to allow internet traffic)

   D (NAT gateway created in private subnet without an internet gateway)

Explanation:

If a private subnet is selected when creating NAT gateway, it cannot route traffic to internet and hence the request would fail. Also, if the security group outbound rules do not allow internet traffic, EC2 cannot download patches from the internet.

7. A (Web server EC2 in public subnet with Elastic IP, RDS in private subnet)

Explanation:

Web server EC2 instance with EIP in public subnet and RDS in private subnet that cannot be reached from the internet, but only can allow traffic from EC2 via security group. From given answers, this looks correct.

8. B (VPN connection from your organization to VPC, Bastion-host in VPN enabled subnet with secure SSH keys to login, EC2 instances in private subnet with secure SSH keys to login, RedShift I private subnet)

Explanation:

VPN connections are used to connect VPCs from your organization's network. Instances that you launch into a VPC can't communicate with your remote network. You can enable access to your remote network from your VPC by attaching a Virtual Private Gateway to the VPC, creating a custom route table, updating your security group rules, and creating an AWS managed VPN connection.

9. **A** (Allow port 22 and SSH protocol on security group inbound, network ACL inbound, network ACL outbound for your IP address)

Explanation:

Security groups are stateful, if you send a request from your instance, the response traffic for that request is allowed to flow regardless of inbound security group rules.

10. **D** (SSH request succeeds due to rule # 100 in NACL inbound and outbound, security group inbound rule)

Explanation:

Security groups are stateful, responses to allowed inbound traffic are allowed to flow out, regardless of outbound rules.

Network ACLs are stateless; responses to allowed inbound traffic are subject to outbound rules

11. **B** (SSH request will be successful because of inbound rule # 100)

Explanation:

A network ACL consists of numbered list of rules that are evaluated in order, starting with the lowest numbered rule. As soon as the rule matches traffic, its applied regardless of any higher-numbered rule that may oppose it.

12. **A** (All requests except HTTPS (443) will fail)

Explanation:

Network ACLs are stateless; responses to inbound traffic are subject to the rules for outbound traffic (or vice versa). In the given case, the outbound rule * denies all the traffic except for 22 and 443, so all the requests will fail.

13. **D** (Setup an S3 proxy on EC2 instance within VPC and transfer data through VPN and S3 proxy to S3)

Explanation:

VPC gateway endpoints are not supported outside VPC. Endpoint connections cannot be extended out of a VPC. So, to support the kind of use cases in the question, we can setup S3 proxy server on EC2 instance.

14. **B** (Subnet's NACL inbound rules does not allow traffic from S3)

      D (EC2 instance security group outbound rules are restricted and does not contain prefix list)

Explanation:

By default, NACLs allow all inbound and outbound traffic. If your NACL rules restrict traffic, you must specify the CIDR block for Amazon S3. The other reason could be because of the VPC security groups; they allow all outbound traffic unless you specifically restrict it.

15. C (Using another VPC NAT gateway is not supported in AWS)

Explanation:

In a VPC peering connection, using NAT gateway of another VPC becomes transitive routing that is not supported in AWS.

16. B (Peered VPCs are in different regions)

Explanation:

AWS supports cross-region VPC peering, so this could not be a reason for failure.

17. C (AWS reserves 5 IP addresses of every subnet)

Explanation:

Amazon reserves the first four and the last one IP address of every subnet for IP networking.

18. D (Enable DNS hostnames for VPC)

Explanation:

By default, custom VPCs do not have DNS hostnames enabled. So, when you launch an EC2 instance in custom VPC, you do not have private DNS name.

19. C (Add secondary CIDR range for the VPC, create new subnet and setup all instances in the same subnet)

Explanation:

You can associate secondary IPv4 CIDR blocks with your VPC. When you associate a new CIDR block with your VPC, a route is automatically added to your VPC route table to enable routing within the VPC.

20. B (VPC B route table contains route with destination as 10.10.1.0/24 and VPC A contains route with destination as 10.11.1.0/28)

Explanation:

To send private IPv4 traffic from your instance to an instance in a peer VPC, you must add a route to the route table that's associated with your subnet in which your instance resides. The route points to the CIDR block of the peer VPC in the VPC peering connection.

21. **C** (Make custom route table as main route table. New subnets created will now simply associate with it)

Explanation:

A custom route table can be designated as main route table. So that, all implicit associations of subnets will now point to the newly set main route table. All future associations of subnets will also point to the new main table.

22. **D** (Create VPC flow log for subnet where RDS instance is launched)

Explanation:

VPC flow logs capture IP traffic going to and from network interfaces in your VPC. Flow log data is stored using Amazon CloudWatch logs. After you have created a flow log, you can view and retrieve its data in CloudWatch logs.

23. **D** (All rules are correct)

Explanation:

Rules are configured correctly without any duplication.

24. **A** (Secondary IP CIDR range 30.0.0.0/20 for VPC with local route)

Explanation:

You can associate secondary IPv4 CIDR blocks with your VPC. When you associate a CIDR block with your VPC, a route is automatically added to your VPC route tables to enable routing within the VPC (the destination is CIDR block and the target is local).

25. **A** (Create a flow log for subnet 10.10.55.0/24)

Explanation:

You can create a flow log for a VPC, a subnet, or a network interface. A VPC flow log captures IP traffic going to and from network in your VPC.

26. **A** (Versioning is enabled)

    C (Transfer acceleration is enabled)

    D (Encryption is enabled)

Explanation:

When you create an S3 bucket, encryption, transfer acceleration and versioning are suspended by default.

27. **C** (Object level logging)

    D (Server access logging)

Explanation:

Following are S3 bucket properties:

Versioning, Server access logging, Static website hosting, Object level logging, Tags, Transfer acceleration, Events.

28. **C** (AWS provides eventual consistency for DELETES)

Explanation:

Amazon S3 provides eventual consistency for overwrite PUTS and DELETES in all regions.

29. **C** (S3 is suitable for immediate downloads because AWS provides Read-After-Write consistency)

    Explanation:

    Amazon S3 provides Read-After-Write consistency for PUTS of new objects in your S3 bucket in all regions with one caveat. The caveat is that if you make a HEAD or GET request to the key name before creating the object. Amazon S3 provides eventual consistency for Read-After-Write

30. **C** (File gateway)

Explanation:

The file gateway presents a file interface that enables you to store files as objects in Amazon S3 using the industry-standard NFS and SMB file protocols, and access the files via NFS or SMB from your data center or Amazon EC2 or access those files as objects with S3 API.

31. **B** (Generate pre signed URL with an expiry date and share the URL with all persons via email)

Explanation:

All objects by default are private, only the object owner has permission to access these objects. The object owner can optionally share objects with others by creating pre signed URL, using own security credentials to grant limited time permission to download the objects.

32. **A** (S3 provides eventual consistency for overwrite PUTS and DELETES)

      B (S3 might return prior data when a process replaces an existing object and immediately attempts to read)

      C (A successful response to a PUT request for new object only occurs when the object is completely saved)

Explanation:

The AWS read-after-write consistency model and eventual consistency model proves our selected three options.

33. **B** (Add a random prefix to the key names)

Explanation:

When your workload is a mix of request types, introduce some randomness to key names by adding a hash string as a prefix to the key names.

34. **D** (With a single PUT operation, you can upload objects up to 5 GB. Use multi-part upload for larger file uploads)

Explanation:

AWS recommends using multi-part upload for larger objects.

35. **B** (Bucket might have a policy with deny and EC2 role is not whitelisted)

      D (Pre signed URLs expired)

Explanation:

While generating pre signed URLs programmatically, we give a duration for the URL to be valid. When the URL is accessed after the specified duration, user will get an error.

You must whitelist all the IAM resources that need access on the bucket if a bucket policy contains an effect as Deny.

36. B (Enable CloudTrail logging using OPTIONS object)

    C (Enable server logging)

Explanation:

Server access logging provides detailed records for the requests that are made to a bucket. Logging is useful for many applications.

37. C (Information of number of requests during peak time)

    D (Information of high availability of data and frequency of requests to choose storage class of objects in S3)

Explanation:

S3 offers different storage classes. Based on the storage type, availability percentage changes along with cost.

38. A (x – amz – meta – location)

    C (x – amz – version – id)

    D (x – amz – server – side – encryption)

Explanation:

AWS bucket objects contain two kinds of metadata, system metadata and user defined metadata. System metadata; such as storage class configured for the object or whether the object has server side encryption enabled, are examples of system metadata.

39. D (Bucket user defined policy is not allowing log delivery group write into S3 bucket)

Explanation:

Server access logging provides detailed records for the requests that are made to a bucket. Server access logs are useful for many applications and these are very useful for security and access audits.

40. C (Add configuration in S3 bucket CORS to allow PUT requests from web application URL)

Explanation:

Cross-Region-Resource-Sharing (CORS) defines a way for client web applications that are loaded in one domain to interact with resources in a different domain. With CORS support,

you can build rich client-side web applications with Amazon S3 and selectively allow cross-region access to your S3 resources.

41. **B** (Either 'name' or 'phone' or no result)

Explanation:

Amazon S3 offers eventual consistency for overwrite PUTS and DELETES. Which means, until the change is fully propagated, S3 might return prior data.

42. **B** (https://s3.us-west-1.amazonaws.com/mybucket)

    C (https://s3-us-west-1.amazonaws.com/mybucket)

    E (https://mybucket.s3-us-west-1.amazonaws.com)

Explanation:

Option E matches virtual-hosted-style URL and it is correct. Option C matches the path-style URL and it is correct. Option D does not match any URL patterns but it is working. You can access the bucket by using this URL.

43. **A** (0 bytes and 5 Terra-Bytes)

Explanation:

The total volume and number of objects that can be stored in S3 are unlimited. Individual objects can range in size from a minimum of 0 bytes to a maximum of 5 terra bytes. The largest object that be uploaded in a single PUT is 5 Giga-bytes.

44. **D** (Set object storage class to Standard-IA. Use lifecycle management to move data from Standard-IA to Glacier after 60 days)

Explanation:

Standard-IA offers cheaper storage than Standard class. IA stands for Infrequently Accessed and in the given scenario, it is mentioned that the data that we are talking about is not accessed on regular basis.

45. **C** (Charges 1 GB for 25 days 5 GB for 11 days)

Explanation:

When versioning is enabled on an S3 bucket, whenever a new version is added to an existing object, keep in mind that older version still remains and AWS charges same price for old and new versions

46. C (Delete the delete marker on the object)

Explanation:

When you delete an object in a versioning enabled bucket, all versions remain in the bucket and Amazon S3 creates a delete marker for the object. To undelete the object, you must delete the delete marker.

47. C (Delete API call does not delete the actual object but only places a delete marker on it)

Explanation:

When versioning is enabled, a simple Delete cannot permanently delete an object.

48. C (Use S3 event notification and configure SNS which sends email to subscribed email address)

   D (Use S3 event function and configure Lambda function which sends email using SES non-sandbox)

Explanation:

The Amazon S3 notification feature enables you to receive notifications when certain events happen in your bucket. To enable notifications, you must first add a notification configuration identifying the events that you want S3 to publish, and the destinations where you want to send these S3 notifications.

49. B (Enable transfer acceleration feature of S3 that improves upload and download speed by using edge locations

   D (Use CloudFront for improving the performance by caching static files on website)

Explanation:

CloudFront can be used to improve performance where network latency is an issue. Amazon S3 Transfer acceleration enables fast, easy, and secure transfer of files over long distances by taking advantage of globally distributed AWS edge locations.

50. A (Yes, on both source and destination buckets)

Explanation:

Cross region replication is a bucket level configuration that enables automatic, asynchronous copying of objects across buckets in different AWS regions. We refer to these buckets as source and destination buckets. These can be owned by different AWS accounts.

51. **D** (Open port 22 (SSH) on EC2 security group and port 2049 (NFS) on EFS security group)

Explanation:

EFS does not require any other port to be opened except 2049 (NFS) on its security group.

52. **B** (Big data and analytics, media processing workflows, content management, web serving, and home directories)

 E (Up to thousands of EC2 instances, from multiple AZs, can connect concurrently to a file system)

Explanation:

Options B and E are characteristics of EFS. All other options are characteristics of Amazon EBS (Elastic Block Store)

53. **A** (Enable encryption during mounting on EC2 using Amazon EFS mount helper. Unmount un-encrypted mount and remount using mount helper encryption during transit option)

Explanation:

AWS provides an option to encrypt data at transit through NFS to EFS.

54. **C** (You will create encryption-at-rest EFS, copy data from old EFS to new EFS and delete the old one)

Explanation:

AWS EFS supports encrypting data at rest, but it can only be done during EFS creation.

55. **A** (EFS mount target security group inbound rules does not allow traffic from new EC2 instances)

Explanation:

EFS provides scalable file storage for use with Amazon EC2. You can create an EFS file system and configure your instance to mount the file system. You can use an EFS file system as a common data source for workloads and applications running on multiple instances.

56. **C** (Peer both VPCs, launch C5 or M5 EC2 instances on new VPC and mount existing EFS on new EC2 instances)

Explanation:

A VPC peering connection is a networking connection between two VPCs that enables you to route traffic between them using private IP addresses.

57. **B** (VPC B's EC2 instance types are not M5 or C5)

   C (Security groups on mount targets do not have NFS port open to VPC B's EC2 instance)

   D (VPC B could be in a different region than VPC A)

Explanation:

EFS does not support request over cross region peered VPCs. Inbound rule for NFS port must be added on mount target's security group for the EC2 instance which will mount the EFS.

58. **C** (Performance mode = General purpose, provides low latency access to EFS)

Explanation:

Although Max I/O is recommended to be used when tens, hundreds or thousands of EC2 instances sharing same EFS, it can slightly increase the latency. In this case, the question states the latency need to be as low as possible.

59. **B** (Throughput mode = Provisioned, you can configure specific throughput irrespective of EFS data size)

Explanation:

With bursting throughput mode, throughput on Amazon EFS scales as a file system grows.

60. **A** (Performance mode = Max I/O, provides higher levels of aggregate throughput and operations per second with a tradeoff of slightly higher latencies)

Explanation:

File systems in the Max I/O mode can scale higher level of aggregate throughputand operations per second with a tradeoff of slightly higher latencies for file operations. Highly

parallelized applications and workloads, such as big data analysis, media processing, and genomics analysis, can benefit from this mode.

61. **C** (Enable access logging)

Explanation:

To help debug issues related to request execution or client access to your API, you can enable CloudWatch logs.

62. **C** (Configure your customer's IP address ranges in resource policy)

   D (Enable CORS and add required host names under access control allow origin)

Explanation:

See documentation for controlling access to an API in API gateway

https://docs.aws.amazon.com/apigateway/latest/developerguide/welcome.html

63. **D** (Stage's Get/users method throttle settings might have overwritten stage throttle settings with burst as 5000 requests)

Explanation:

You can override stage settings on an individual method within a stage.

64. **B** (Enable API caching to serve frequently requested data from API cache)

   D (Enable throttling and control the number of requests per second)

Explanation:

To prevent your API from being overwhelmed by too many requests, API Gateway throttles requests to your API. Specifically, API gateway sets a limit on a steady-state rate and a burst of request submissions against all APIs in your account. Also, you can enable API caching in API gateway to cache your endpoint's responses. With caching, you can reduce the number of calls made to your endpoint and it also improves the latency.

65. **B** (VPC Link)

   D (Lambda functions from another account)

   E (Public facing HTTPS-based endpoints outside AWS network)

Explanation:

API gateway can integrate with any HTTPS-based endpoints available on the internet. Option D is correct because AWS can use Lambda function from another account as an

integration type. For option E, AWS has introduced VPC Link, a way to connect with the resources inside a private VPC.

66. **C** (Use VPC Link to integrate on premise backend solutions through DirectConnect and private VPC)

Explanation:

See documentation for VPC Link

https://aws.amazon.com/blogs/compute/introducing-amazon-api-gateway-private-endpoints/

67. **B** (VPC Route Tables)

   C (Server-side certificates)

Explanation:

API Gateway supports multiple mechanisms for controlling access to your API, which includes: Resource policies, AWS IAM roles and policies, CORS, Lambda authorizers, Amazon cognito user pools, client-side SSL certificates, and usage plans.

68. **B** (Refresh cache)

Explanation:

For information about caching, see aws documentation documentationhttps://docs.aws.amazon.com/apigateway/latest/developerguide/api-gateway-caching.html

69. **B** (Protection from distributed denial-of-service (DDoS) attacks)

Explanation:

API Gateway supports multiple mechanisms for controlling access to your API, which includes: Resource policies, AWS IAM roles and policies, CORS, Lambda authorizers, Amazon cognito user pools, client-side SSL certificates, and usage plans.

70. **A** (5000 requests will succeed and throttles the rest 3000 in one-second period)

Explanation:

To prevent your API from being overwhelmed by too many requests, API gateway throttles requests to your API using token bucket algorithm. Using this algorithm, the burst is the maximum bucket size.

71. **C** (Customers have control over ECS instances and monitoring can be setup like a normal EC2 instance)

Explanation:

AWS ECS uses EC2 instances with ECS optimized AMI. You will have root access to the instance and you can manage them.

72. **C** (Outbound rules of ECS instance's security group are not allowing traffic to ECS service endpoint)

   E (IAM role used to run ECS instance does not have ecs:Poll action in its policy)

Explanation:

The Amazon ECS container agent makes calls to API on your behalf. Container instances that run the agent require an IAM policy and role for the service to know that the agent belongs to you. Before you can launch container instances and register them into a cluster, you must create an IAM role for those container services to use when they are launched.

73. **C** (Set configuration is user data parameter of ECS instance)

Explanation:

When you launch a container instance, you have the option of passing user data to the instance. The data can be used to perform common automated configuration tasks and even run scripts when the instance boots. For ECS, the most common use cases of passing user data are, Docker daemon and ECS container agent.

74. **C** (Check CloudTrail logs)

Explanation:

Amazon ECS is integrated with AWS CloudTrail that provides a record of actions taken by a user, role or an AWS service in Amazon ECS.

75. **A** (IAM role that allows ECS to make calls to your load balancer on your behalf)

   D (Task definition of the task definition to run in your service)

   E (Cluster on which to run your service)

Explanation:

A service definition defines which task definition to use with your service, how many instantiations of that task to run, and which load balancers (if any) to associate with your tasks.

76. **A** (Command that the container should run when it is started)
    C (How much CPU and memory to use with each container)
    E (The Docker images to use with the containers in your task)

Explanation:

See Amazon ECS task definitions

https://docs.aws.amazon.com/AmazonECS/latest/developerguide/task_definitions.html

77. **C** (FARGATE)

Explanation:

For detailed information on ECS launch, see documentation

https://docs.aws.amazon.com/AmazonECS/latest/developerguide/launch_types.html

78. **D** (JSON template that describes containers which forms your application)

Explanation:

How to create task definitions, see AWS documentation

https://docs.aws.amazon.com/AmazonECS/latest/developerguide/task_definitions.html

79. **B** (Cluster)
    D (Tasks)
    E (Task definition)

Explanation:

The features for AWS ECS are containers and images, task definitions, tasks and scheduling, clusters, and container agents.

80. **B** (Create a NAT gateway and attach it to VPC subnet's route table in which ECS instance is running)

Explanation:

The container agent runs on each infrastructure resource and sends information about the resource's current running tasks and resource utilization to Amazon ECS, and starts and stops tasks whenever required.

81. **A** (AWS OpsWorks)

  C (AWS CodePipeline)

Explanation:

Supported event sources for Lambda function include; S3, DynamoDB, Kinesis, SNS, SES, SQS, Cognito, CloudFormation, CloudWatch logs, CloudWatch events, CodeCommit, Alexa, AWS Config, Lex, API gateway, IoT button, CloudFront.

82. **D** (Lambda function code)

  E (Providing access to AWS resources which triggers Lambda function)

Explanation:

When using AWS Lambda, you are only responsible for code, and also, Lambda assumes that the role assigned during setup to access any AWS resources it performs actions on it. Policy on the role must grant access to any resources in order for Lambda to perform operations.

83. **C** (Download S3 bucket objects of size varying between 500 MB-2 GB to a Lambda Ephemeral disk or temp location)

Explanation:

Option C looks like a potential use case, but the scenario will fail due to the /tmp directory space limitation

84. **B** (10)

Explanation:

Batch size is the number of records that AWS Lambda will retrieve from each ReceiveMessage call. The default and the maximum batch size supported by SQS is up to 10 queue messages per batch.

85. **A** (Origin response)

  B (Origin request)

  C (Viewer request)

Explanation:

See AWS documentation for CloudFront events that can trigger Lambda@edge function

https://docs.aws.amazon.com/AmazonCloudFront/latest/DeveloperGuide/lambda-cloudfront-trigger-events.html

86. **B** (DynamoDB)
    C (SQS)
    D (Kinesis)

Explanation:

AWS Lambda supports these three poll based services that we have chosen.

87. **B** (arn:aws:lambda:aws-region:acct-id:function:helloworld/PROD)
    D (arn:aws:lambda:aws-region:acct-id:function:helloworld)
    E (arn:aws:lambda:aws-region:acct-id:function:helloworld:$LATEST)

Explanation:

You can refer to the function using its Amazon Resource Name (ARN)

Qualified ARN: The function ARN with the version suffix (option E)

Unqualified ARN: The function ARN without the version suffix (option D)

When using any of the alias ARN, each alias ARN has an alias name suffix (option E)

88. **B** (2112 MB memory and 10 seconds timeout)

Explanation:

AWS Lambda resource limits per invocation stated in the topic in AWS documentation.

89. **C** (AWS SNS)
    E (AWS SNS)

Explanation:

Asynchronously invoked Lambda function is retried twice before the event is discarded. If you don't know the reason of retries getting failed, use Dead-letter Queues (DLQ) to direct unprocessed events to an Amazon SQS queue or Amazon SNS topic to analyze the failure.

90. **C** (logs:CreateLogGroup)
    D (logs:CreateLogStream)
    E (logs:PutLogEvents)

Explanation:

AWSLambdaBasicExecutionRole grants permissions only for the Amazon CloudWatch logs actions to write logs. You can use this policy if your Lambda function does not access any other AWS resources except writing logs.

91. **D** (Memory)

Explanation:

The AWS/Lambda namespace does not include memory in metrics.

92. **C** (With asynchronous invocation, if Lambda is unable to fully process the event and if you don't specify a dead-letter queue, the event will be discarded)

Explanation:

Asynchronous events are queued before being used to invoke the Lambda function. If AWS Lambda is unable to fully process the event, it will automatically retry the invocation twice, with delays in retries.

93. **B** (Use AWS_LAMBDA_FUNCTION_VERSION environment variable)
    D (getFunctionVersion from context object)

Explanation:

getFunctionVersion(): The Lambda function version that is executing. If an alias is used to invoke the function, then getFunctionVersion will be the version the alias points to. For more information on environment variables, check AWS documentation

https://docs.aws.amazon.com/lambda/latest/dg/welcome.html

94. **C** (Use environment variable to pass configuration. Use encryption helpers to encrypt sensitive information by your own KMS key. Decrypt the variable using decryption helper code provided in the console)

Explanation:

For information about storing sensitive information using Lambda, see AWS documentation

https://docs.aws.amazon.com/lambda/latest/dg/env_variables.html?shortFooter=true

95. **B** (/26)

Explanation:

In the given case, ENI capacity would be, 100 * (1 GB / 3 GB) = 30

Out of the given options, /26 is the minimum CIDR block that Lambda function requires to work without any issues.

96. **D** (Add permission for Test account on Dev account's lambda function policy through AWS CLI)

Explanation:

See example use case in AWS documentation

https://docs.aws.amazon.com/lambda/latest/dg/access-control-resource-based.html?shortFooter=true%23access-control-resource-based-example-cross-account-scenario

97. **D** (Create an alias, point it to PROD version and share the ARN with apps. When new version is published, change the alias to point to it)

Explanation:

By using aliases, you can access the lambda function an alias is pointing to.

98. **A** (Requests might be served by old or new version for a brief period of less than one minute)

Explanation:

When you update a lambda function, there will be a brief window of time, typically less than a minute, when requests could be served by either the old or the new version of your function.

99. **C** (Replicate the Java code easily onto lambda function and use lambda invoke API with input passed as custom event)

Explanation:

You can invoke a lambda function using a custom event through lambda's invoke API. Only the function owner or another AWS account that the owner has granted permission can invoke lambda function.

100. **B** (You can set "Constant (JSON text)" option while selecting lambda as trigger for CloudWatch scheduled event)

Explanation:

When using CloudWatch rule to trigger a lambda event, one of the multiple options you have to pass data onto your lambda function is "Constant (JSON Text)." This handy feature allows you to send static content to your function instead of the matched event.

101. **C** (Lambda execution role policy does not have access to create CloudWatch logs)

Explanation:

AWSLambdaKinesisExecutionRole grants permissions for Amazon Kinesis data streams actions, and CloudWatch logs actions. You can attach this permission policy if you are writing a lambda function to process Kinesis stream events.

102. **C** (Lambda function is running in same VPC as RDS, but RDS instance security group is not allowing connections from lambda subnet range)
    D (Lambda function is running in "no VPC" network mode)

Explanation:

When lambda function is running in "no-VPC" network mode, it will not have access to the resources that are running in a private VPC. If there is no inbound rule defined in the security group to allow connections from lambda subnet IP range, connections will fail.

103. **A** (Configure Dead-letter queue (DLQ) and send notification to SNS topic)

Explanation:

You can forward non-processed payloads to DLQ using AWS SQS and SNS.

104. **C** (Lambda function is set to run in a private VPC without NAT gateway or VPC endpoint)

Explanation:

For the lambda function to access S3 service endpoints from inside a private VPC, there should be a NAT gateway or S3 VPC endpoint configured in the route table associated with the subnet that was chosen during the creation of the function.

105. C (Configure DLQ with SQS, configure SQS to trigger lambda function again)

Explanation:

You can forward non processed or failed payloads to Dead Letter Queue (DLQ)

106. **C** (AWS VM Import)

Explanation:

According to AWS documentation; VM Import/Export enables you to easily import virtual machine images from your existing environment to Amazon EC2 instances and export them back to your on premises environment.

107. **B** (DynamoDB)
     C (Lambda)
     D (API Gateway)

Explanation:

Amazon API gateway is a fully managed service that makes it easy to create, publish, maintain, monitor, and secure APIs at any scale. AWS lambda lets you run your code without provisioning or managing servers. DynamoDB is a fully managed NoSQL database service that provides a fast and predictable performance with seamless scalability.

108. **A** (Amazon CloudFront)

Explanation:

CloudFront is a web service that speeds up distribution of your static and dynamic web content; such as, .html, .css, .js, and image files.

109. **C** (VPG)
     D (A hardware compatible VPN device)

Explanation:

When defining a VPN connection between the on premises network and the VPC, you need to have a customer gateway defined. Since this is on the internet, it needs to have a static internet routable IP address.

110. **C** (AWS ELB)
     D (AWS Autoscaling)

Explanation:

You can automatically increase the size of your auto scaling group when demand goes up and decrease it when the demand goes down. The Elastic Load Balancing service automatically routes incoming traffic in such a dynamically changing number of EC2 instances.

111. **C** (Amazon ElastiCache)

Explanation:

ElastiCache offers fully managed Redis and memcached to seamlessly deploy, operate, and scale popular open source compatible in-memory data stores. Build data-intensive apps or improve the performance of existing apps by retrieving data with high throughput and low latency in-memory data stores.

112. **B** (Enable global tables for DynamoDB)

Explanation:

Check the AWS documentation for global tables

https://docs.aws.amazon.com/amazondynamodb/latest/developerguide/GlobalTables.html

113. **C** (CloudWatch)
     D (AWS Trusted Advisor)

Explanation:

CloudWatch is a monitoring and management service for developers, system operators, and IT managers. AWS Trusted advisor is an online resource to help you reduce cost, increase performance, and improve security by optimizing your AWS environment.

114. **C** (Amazon RedShift)

Explanation:

RedShift is a fully managed petabyte-scale data warehouse service in the cloud. You can start with just a few hundred Gigabytes of data and scale to a petabyte or more.

115. **A** (AWS VPC Flow Logs)

Explanation:

VPC Flow logs documentation link is given below

https://docs.aws.amazon.com/vpc/latest/userguide/flow-logs.html

116. **B** (Kinesis)

Explanation:

Kinesis data streams enables you to build custom apps that process or analyze streaming data for specialized needs. You can continuously add various types of data such as, clickstreams, application logs, and social media to an Amazon Kinesis data stream from hundreds or thousands of sources.

117. **B** (Elastic Container Service)

Explanation:

Amazon ECS is a highly scalable, fast container service that makes it easy to run, stop, and manage Docker containers for a cluster of Amazon EC2 instances.

118. **C** (CloudFront)

Explanation:

Edge optimized APIs are endpoints that are accessed through a CloudFront distribution created and managed by API Gateway.

119. **C** (Security groups)
     D (NACLs)

Explanation:

A security group acts as a virtual firewall for your instance to control inbound and outbound traffic, a Network Access Control List is an optional layer of security for your VPC that acts as a firewall for controlling traffic in and out of one or more subnets.

120.   **B** (API CORS)

Explanation:

When your API's resources receive requests from a domain other than the API's own domain, you must enable cross-region resource sharing (CORS) for selected methods on the resource.

121. **B** (2 servers in each of AZs through e, inclusive)

Explanation:

The best way is to distribute the instances across multiple AZs to get the best performance and to avoid a disaster scenario. For more information on high availability and fault-tolerance, follow the link below

https://media.amazonwebservices.com/architecturecenter/AWS_ac_ra_ftha_04.pdf

122.   **C** (Copy the AMI from Singapore to Asia region, modify the auto scaling groups in the backup region to use the new AMI ID in the backup region)

Explanation:

If you need an AMI across multiple regions, you have to copy it across regions. Note that; by default, AMIs that you have created will not be available across all regions.

123.   **A** (S3 to store ELB log files and EMR for processing these files in the analysis)

Explanation:

If you see "collection and processing of logs," directly think of AWS EMR. EMR provides a managed Hadoop framework that makes it easy, fast, and cost-effective to process the vast amount of data.

124.   **B** (Develop each app in a separate Docker container and deploy using Elastic BeanStalk)

Explanation:

Elastic BeanStalk supports the deployment of web applications from Docker containers. With Docker containers, you can define your runtime environment. You can choose your platform, programming language, and application dependencies that aren't supported by any other platform.

125.   **C** (Store logs in S3, use lifecycle policies to archive Amazon Glacier)

Explanation:

Check AWS documentation for lifecycle management

https://docs.aws.amazon.com/AmazonS3/latest/dev/object-lifecycle-mgmt.html

126.   **D** (CloudTrail for security logs)

Explanation:

CloudTrail is an AWS service to monitor all the API calls and is used for logging and monitoring for compliance purpose.

127.   **A** (Create an IAM role that allows write access to the DynamoDB table)

Explanation:

Delegate permissions to make API calls using IAM roles instead of disturbing your AWS credentials.

128.   **D** (Add tags to the instances marking each environment then segregate access using IAM policies)

Explanation:

Tags enable you to categorize your AWS resources in different ways. This is useful when you have many resources of the same type. You can quickly identify a resource based on its tags.

129.   **D** (AWS DynamoDB)

Explanation:

DynamoDB is a fully managed NoSQL database service which enables customers to offload the administrative burdens of operating and scaling distributed databases to AWS, so they don't have to worry about hardware provisioning, setup, and configuration, throughput planning, replication, software planning, or cluster scaling.

130.   **C** (AWS EMR)

Explanation:

Amazon EMR securely and reliably handles a broad set of big data use cases, including log analysis, web indexing, data transformations (ETL), machine learning, financial analysis, scientific simulation, and bioinformatics.

131. **A** (Set up the public website on a public subnet and set up the database in a private subnet which connects to the internet via a NAT instance)

Explanation:

VPC scenarios for public and private subnets are described in the following link

https://docs.aws.amazon.com/vpc/latest/userguide/VPC_Scenario2.html

132.   **B** (Create a service that pulls SQS messages and writes these to DynamoDB to handle sudden spikes in DynamoDB)

Explanation:

When looking for scalability, SQS is the best option. DynamoDB is scalable, but since a cost-effective solution is required, SQS messaging can assist in managing the mentioned situation.

133.**B** (Disable automated and manual snapshots on the cluster)

Explanation:

Snapshots are point-in-time backups of a cluster and are of two types, i.e., manual and automated. RedShift stores these snapshots internally in S3 by using an encrypted SSL connection. Since the question already mentions that the data is reproducible, you do not need to maintain snapshots.

134.   **C** (Create and origin access identity (OAI) for CloudFront and grant access to the objects in your S3 bucket to that OAI)

Explanation:

If users directly access your objects in S3, they bypass the controls provided by CloudFront signed URLs or signed cookies. Also, if users access objects both through CloudFront and directly by using S3 URLs, CloudFront access logs are less useful.

135.   **B** (Shard your data set among multiple Amazon RDS DB instances)
        C (Use EalstiCache in front of your RDS instance to cache common queries)
        F (Add DB read replicas, and have your application direct read queries to them)

Explanation:

Amazon RDS read replicas provide enhanced performance and durability for database instances. Sharding is a common concept to split data across multiple tables in a database. ElastiCache improves the performance if web applications by allowing you to retrieve information from fast, managed, in-memory data stores, instead of relying on slower disk-based databases.

136.   **A** (Use the ECR service to store the Docker images)

Explanation:

Amazon Elastic Container Registry (ECR) is a fully managed Docker container registry that makes it easy for developers to store, manage, and deploy Docker container images.

137. **C** (Use the Elastic BeanStalk service to provision the environment)

Explanation:

Elastic BeanStalk is an easy to use service for deploying and scaling web applications and services developed with Java, .NET, PHP, Node.js, Python, Ruby, Go, and Docker on familiar servers such Apache, Nginx, Passenger, and IIS.

138. **B** (Data records are only accessible for a default time of 24 hours)

Explanation:

A Kinesis stream is an ordered sequence of data records meant to be written to and read from in real-time. The time period for when a record is added to when it is no longer accessible is called the retention period. A Kinesis stream stores record from 24 hours by default, up to 168 hours.

139. **D** (EBS Provisioned IOPS SSD)

Explanation:

Since this is a high-performance requirement with high IOPS needed, one should opt for Provisioned IOPS SSD.

140. **C** (Use a hexadecimal hash for the prefix)

Explanation:

One way to introduce randomness to key name is to add a hash string as a prefix to the key name.

141. **D** (Amazon RedShift)

Explanation:

Amazon RedShift is a column-oriented, fully managed, petabyte-scale data warehouse that makes it simple and cost-effective to analyze all your data using your existing business intelligent tools. Amazon RedShift achieves efficient storage and optimum query performance through a combination of massively parallel processing, columnar data storage, and very efficient, targeted data compression encoding schemes.

142. **C** (AWS SQS)

Explanation:

The Simple Queue Service can be used to build a decoupled architecture.

143. **A** (Use NAT Gateway in the public subnet)

Explanation:

The AWS documentation states that the NAT gateway is highly available and requires less maintenance.

https://docs.aws.amazon.com/vpc/latest/userguide/vpc-nat-comparison.html

144. **A** (Weighted)

Explanation:

As per AWS documentation, the weighted routing policy is good for testing new versions of software, and it is the ideal approach for Blue-Green deployments.

145. **A** (Use VPC peering)

Explanation:

A VPC peering connection is a networking connection between two VPCs that enables you to route traffic between them privately. Instances in either VPC can communicate with each other as if they are within the same network. You can create a peering connection between your VPCs, with a VPC in another account, or with a VPC in a different region.

146. **B** (EBS Throughput Optimized)

Explanation:

While considering storage volume types for batch processing activities with large throughput, consider using the EBS Throughput Optimized volume type.

147. **B** (Lambda)

Explanation:

AWS Lambda is a compute service that lets you run code without provisioning and managing servers.

148. **C** (Don't save your API credentials, instead, create an IAM role and assign this role to an EC2 instance when you first create it)

Explanation:

IAM roles are designed so that your apps can securely make API requests from your instances, without requiring you to manage the security credentials.

149. **D** (AWS SNS)

Explanation:

Amazon Simple Notification Service (SNS) is a web service that coordinates and manages the delivery or sending of messages to subscribing endpoints.

150. **B** (Trusted Advisor)

Explanation:

The Trusted Advisor can monitor services EC2 and EBS with some limits that are listed in the AWS documentation.

https://aws.amazon.com/premiumsupport/ta-faqs/

151. **B** (CloudWatch)

Explanation:

CloudWatch metrics help you monitor physical aspects of your cluster, such as CPU utilization, latency, and throughput. Metric data is displayed directly in the Amazon RedShift console. You can also view it in in the Amazon CloudWatch console.

152. **D** (SSE-S3)

Explanation:

According to the documentation published by AWS, SSE-S3 manages the data and the master encryption keys.

153. **D** (Place the S3 bucket behind a CloudFront distribution)

Explanation:

Using CloudFront can be more cost-effective if your users access your objects frequently because, at higher usage, the price for CloudFront data transfer is lower than the price for S3 data transfer.

154.   **A** (Create an AMI of the EC2 instance and copy it to another region)

Explanation:

You can copy an AMI within or across an AWS region using AWS management console, the CLI, the SDKs, or the EC2 API, all of which support the CopyImage action.

155.   **C** (Use transition rule in S3 to move the files to Glacier and use expiration rule to delete it after 30 days)

Explanation:

Lifecycle configuration enables you to specify the lifecycle management of objects in a bucket. The configuration is a set of one or more rules that define an action for S3 to apply to a group of objects.

156.   **D** (Glacier)

Explanation:

Amazon Glacier is an extremely low-cost storage service that provides durable storage with security features for data archiving and backup.

157.   **B** (DynamoDB)

Explanation:

Amazon DynamoDB is a fully managed NoSQL database service that lets you offload the administrative burdens of operating and scaling a distributed database. You don't have to worry about hardware provisioning, setup, and configuration, replication, software patching, or cluster scaling.

158.   **B** (The replication is lagging)

Explanation:

Read replicas are separate database instances that are replicated asynchronously. As a result, they are subject to replication lag and might be missing some of the latest transactions.

159.   **A** (Provisioned IOPS for the database server)
        D (General Purpose SSD for the web server)

Explanation:

It is mentioned that the database will receive a lot of read/write requests, the ideal solution is to have the underlying EBS volume as Provisioned IOPS. In the case of standard workload, GP2 will be sufficient.

160.   **A** (Place a CloudFront distribution in front of the EC2 instance)

Explanation:

It is mentioned that there is only one EC2 instance, so placing it behind a load balancer doesn't make any sense. CloudFront would help alleviate the load because of its edge location and cache features.

161. **C** (An IAM role with required permissions)

Explanation:

While working with lambda functions, if you are in need of accessing other resources, make sure that an IAM role is in place.

162.   **C** (Updates are being made to the same key for the object)

Explanation:

Updates made to objects in S3 follow an eventual consistency model. Therefore, for object updates made to the same key, there can be a slight delay when the updated object is provided back to the user on the next read request.

163.   **B** (AWS OpsWorks)

Explanation:

AWS OpsWorks stacks and AWS OpsWorks for Chef Automate let you use Chef cookbooks and solutions for configuration management.

164.   **D** (Use security groups)

Explanation:

Security groups can be used to control traffic into an EC2 instance.

165.   **C** (There is no need to do anything as logs are automatically encrypted)

Explanation:

By default, CloudTrail event log files are encrypted using S3 server-side encryption (SSE).

166.   **C** (Put an ElastiCache in front of the database)

Explanation:

The ideal solution would be to use ElastiCache because it provides a high performance, scalable, and cost-effective caching solution. It also removes the complexity associated with deploying and managing a distributed cache environment.

167.   **B** (Enable versioning on the S3 bucket)
       C (Enable MFA delete on the S3 bucket)

Explanation:

When a user performs a DELETE operation on an object, subsequent simple (un-versioned) requests will no longer retrieve the object. Versioning's MFA delete capability can be used to provide an additional layer of security, When MFA delete is enabled on an S3 bucket, two forms of authentication are required to permanently delete a version of an object.

168.   **D** (Aurora)

Explanation:

According to AWS documentation, Aurora is a drop-in replacement for MySQL and PostgreSQL. The code, tools, and applications that you use with your existing MySQL and PostgreSQL databases can be used with Amazon Aurora.

169.   **A** (Standard retrieval)

Explanation:

Standard retrievals are a cost-effective way of accessing your data within just a few hours. You can use standard retrievals to restore backup data, retrieve archived media content for same-day editing or distribution, or pull and analyze logs to drive business decisions within hours.

170.   **D** (S3)

Explanation:

S3 is the perfect place to store documents. You can define buckets for each user and have policies to restrict access so that each user can only access his/her files.

171. **D** (Use the API gateway and provide integration with lambda functions)

Explanation:

API Gateway provides ideal access to your backend system and services via API.

172.   **C** (Add randomness to the key names)
        D (Add a CloudFront distribution in front of the bucket)

Explanation:

When your workload is sending mostly GET requests, you can add randomness to the key names. In addition, you can integrate CloudFront with S3 to distribute content to your users.

173.   **D** (Take regular EBS snapshots)

Explanation:

You can back up the data on Amazon EBS volumes y taking point-in-time snapshots. These are incremental backups which means that only the blocks that have changed after your most-recent snapshot are saved.

174.   **D** (Delete the manual snapshots)

Explanation:

With automated snapshots enabled, you can still take manual snapshots at any time. RedShift will not delete any manual snapshots. Manual snapshots retain even if you delete the cluster.

175.   **B** (Use storage gateway stored volumes)

Explanation:

AWS storage gateway connects an on-premises system with cloud storage to integrate both with data security features.

176.   **D** (Add this entry to route table: 0.0.0.0/0 -> internet gateway)

Explanation:

The route table needs to be modified with the selected entry to make sure that the routes from the internet reach the instance. When we add this to the route table, all other options become invalid.

177. **C** (Set up your app on more EC2 instances and set them behind an ELB)
D (Set up your app on more EC2 instances and use Route 53 to route requests accordingly)

Explanation:

The elastic load balancer can be used to distribute traffic to EC2 instances. So, to add elasticity, one can either use an ELB or Route 53. Route 53 can setup routing policies to distribute requests to multiple EC2 instances.

178. **A** (Use ECS service for Kubernetes)

Explanation:

Amazon ECS service for Kubernetes (EKS) automates the deployment, scaling, and management of containerized applications.

179. **C** (Add the scripts for the installation in the user data section)
D (Create a golden image and then create a launch configuration)

Explanation:

The user data section of an instance launch can be used to pre-configure software after the instance is initially booted. Also, you can create an AMI or a golden image with the already installed software. The auto-scaling group can use your provided launch configuration.

180. **C** (S3 for storing the log files and EMR for processing the log files)

Explanation:

Amazon EMR is a managed cluster platform that simplifies running big data frameworks. EMR can be used to transform and move a large amount of data into and out of other AWS stores and databases, such as S3 and DynamoDB.

181. **B** (Spot instances)

Explanation:

Spot instances let you bid on unused EC2 instances. This lowers the cost significantly.

182. **B** (Use CloudFormation to spin up resources in another region if a disaster occurs in the primary region)

Explanation:

The focus is on cost minimization. Therefore, the best approach is to create CloudFormation templates which can be used to spin up resources in another region during disaster recovery.

183.   **C** (EC2)
       D (ELB)

Explanation:

The AWS Whitepaper for well architecture framework, states that: The following services can be deployed to multiple availability zones; multiple regions if required for distributing workload across multiple availability zones and AWS regions.

184.   **C** (DynamoDB)

Explanation:

To study about the stateless architectures, follow this link

https://aws.amazon.com/whitepapers/architecting-for-the-aws-cloud-best-practices/

185.   **B** (Enable cross-region replication for the bucket)

Explanation:

Cross-region replication is a bucket level configuration that enables automatic, asynchronous copying of objects across buckets in different AWS regions.

186.   **C** (Add a scheduled scaling policy at 7:30 AM)
       Explanation:
       Scaling based on scheduled helps you to scale an application in response to predictable load modifications so that capacity is high before 8:30 AM.

187.   **C** (Upload static content to an S3 bucket)
       D (Enable website hosting for an S3 bucket)
       Explanation:
       According to the given condition, the most cost-effective and ideal solution is S3 because in S3 you can host a static website in which individual web pages include static content.

188.   **D** (Create an Alias record which points to the CloudFront distribution)
       Explanation:

Standard DNS records are Amazon Route53 records while alias records give extensions to DNS functionality. Alias record contains a pointer to multiple services like CloudFront distribution as a static website or another Route 53 record in the same hosted zone.

189.   **D** (Create an Elastic Beanstalk environment with necessary Docker containers)
       Explanation:
       Elastic Beanstalk can be used to host Docker container, and with the help of a Docker container you can also define your runtime environment

190.   **C** (Remove public read access and use signed URLs with expiry dates)
       Explanation:
       With the help of pre-signed URL, you can define which user/customer can upload an object to your bucket. Initially, all the objects and bucket are private. They are valid for some specific duration.

191.   **A** (AWS DynamoDB)
       Explanation:
       Amazon DynamoDB is a fully managed NoSQL database service that provides fast and predictable performance with seamless scalability.

192.   **B** (AWS Lambda) **and c** (AWS API gateway)
       Explanation:
       AWS lambda and API gateway both are a serverless component that allows you to build independent services and for managing access to API's respectively

193.   **C** (Use AWS Cloudwatch metrics and logs to watch errors)
       Explanation:
       With the help of Amazon CloudWatch, AWS Lambda monitors Lambda functions automatically on your behalf, and store logs through Amazon CloudWatch log automatically.

194.   **C** (Enable cross-region replication for an S3 bucket)
       Explanation:
       By default data store in S3 across multiple geographical distant AZ. To support compliance requirement cross-region replication allows you to replicate data between distant AWS regions.

195. **A** (Store the file in Amazon S3 and create lifecycle policy to remove the file after one year)
Explanation:
Lifecycle configuration enables lifecycle management of an object in a bucket. Configuration consist of rules and each rule has actions for Amazon S3 to apply to a group of the object.
Action #1 is transit action in which you define transition of an object into other storage class.
Action #2 is expiration action in which you define when the object is expired, and then Amazon S3 deletes that object on your behalf.

196. **A** (Amazon Cloudwatch) **and d** (Amazon Simple notification service)
Explanation:
Amazon Cloud watch is used to monitor Metric from RDS instances, and to send a notification Amazon Simple Notification service is used.

197. **A** (EBS Cold HDD)
Explanation:
Cold HDD volumes are ideal for storage of less frequent access data at low cost.

198. **C** (Have another EC2 instance in another availability zone with replication configuration)
Explanation:
For high availability, you have the EC2 Instance in another Availability Zone so in case if any AZ fails the other one is available.

199. **D** (Changes applied to security group and application should be able to respond to 443 requests)
Explanation:
When you add rules in the security group, they automatically applied to all instances associated to that security group because security group is setting up a firewall on destination port rather than source port.

200. **A** (Ensure the right route entry in the route table)
Explanation:

Make sure that the internet gateway must be added in the route table so instances can communicate over the internet.

201. **B** (Amazon CloudWatch Logs) **and d** (Amazon CloudTrail)
Explanation:
AWS CloudTrail is a service to continuously monitor and logs the account activity across your infrastructure and Amazon CloudWatch logs are used to monitor, store and access logs file from EC2 instances and other sources.

202. **B** (Ensure that right instance class is chosen for critical data) **and d** (Encrypt database during the creation)
Explanation:
Encryption in the database needs to be done during its creation because at rest it is not possible and also assures about that underlying instance type supports DB encryption.

203. **C** (Ensure IAM role is attached to the Lambda function which has required DynamoDB privileges)
Explanation:
You need to define IAM role when you create an AWS Lambda function to grant permission to this role.
   ✓ If other AWS services are accessed by AWS Lambda function code such as reading or writing, you need to grant permissions for related AWS service actions to the role.
   ✓ If the event source is stream-based (Amazon Kinesis Data Streams and DynamoDB streams). AWS Lambda needs permissions to poll the stream and read new records on the stream, so they need to grant permissions to this role.

204. **B** (Amazon EBS provisioned IOPS SSD)
Explanation:
In the question, it is stated that application is frequently used for high read and write operation. So, in that case, Provisioned IOPS SSD is the best option. They are designed for the intensive workload.

205. **D** (Use NAT gateway instead of NAT instance)
Explanation:

Instead of Nat instance, you can use NAT gateway as a managed resource because changing type of NAT instance will not give a guarantee that the issue will not occur again.

206. **C** (Spot Instances)
Explanation:
Like batch processing job in which jobs don't last for an entire year it can be allocated and deallocated as per request similarly above scenario is that. So, for this spot instance is the best type to choose.

207. **A** (Create a geolocation Route53 policy to route the policy based on locations)
Explanation:
When you want to route traffic depending upon the location of your users which means a location that DNS queries originate from.

208. **C** (Ensure that the security group allows inbound SSH traffic from the administrator's workstation)
Explanation:
As we know that security groups are stateful so there is no need of configuration for outbound traffic because whatever traffic is allowed through inbound it is also allowed for outbound too.

209. **B** (Amazon EBS volumes)
Explanation:
An Amazon EBS volume is block-level storage which can be attached to a single EC2 instance. It is also used as primary storage.

210. **C** (Attach an internet gateway to VPC and add a route for 0.0.0.0/0 to the route table)
Explanation:
When you need to access an instance from the internet, you need to attach internet gateway to VPC with route 0.0.0.0/0 to the route table.

211. **D** (Amazon S3 will automatically manage performance at this scale)
Explanation:

Amazon S3 increases read and write request exponentially and automatically scales to high request rates.

212. **B** (Organization create scripts which can be added to the user data section when the instance is launched)
Explanation:
After launching EC2 instance, you can pass user data to EC2 instance to perform common automated configuration tasks, or you can even run scripts.

213. **A (8)**
Explanation:
Each subnet is correlated to one availability zone and according to requirement 4 AZ for both application and web server which means you need eight subnets.

214. **D** (Use Route53 with failover option to a static S3 website bucket or CloudFront distribution)
Explanation:
Multiple resources that perform the same function then configure DNS failover to route53, so it shifts your traffic from unhealthy resources to healthy resources. So you can route traffic to a website hosted on S3 or to a CloudFront distribution.

215. **B** (Attach an Internet Gateway to VPC and route is to the subnet)
Explanation:
The instance is not accessible until internet gateway is not attached to VPC to access the instance from the internet.

216. **A** (Use IAM user roles) **and b** (Use bucket policies)
Explanation:
When access policies are attached to resources like bucket and objects then it is resource based policies, if access policies attach to the user, then it is user policies.

217. **C** (Use Fargate launch type in AWS ECS)
Explanation:
With the help of Fargate, you can run the containerized application without providing backend infrastructure. When you register the task, it simply launches the container.

218. **B** (Define the tags on the test and planning servers and add a condition to IAM policy with allows access to specific tags)
Explanation:
With the help of tags, you can easily control access via IAM policy. By defining conditions.

219. **D** (Use SQS Queues to Queue the database writes)
Explanation:
According to given scenario, you can use SQS queue to store pending write request, which gives surety to the delivery of these messages and SQS handles 120000 messages inflight because more IOPS will help to eliminate the chance of losing data.

220. **B** (Enable Versioning for an S3 bucket)
Explanation:
In S3, versioning is at bucket level and used to recover prior versions of an object

221. **C** (Use AWS storage gateway-cached volumes service)
Explanation:
To extend your on-premises storage Gateway, the cached volume is best because it gives frequent access to data with low latency although Amazon S3 is the primary storage. Create storage volumes and attach them as iSCSI devices from on-premises application servers then the data written in volume gateway stores it in Amazon S3 and keeping recent read data in on-premises storage gateway cache.

222. **B** (Consider using VPC endpoint)
Explanation:
A VPC endpoint connects you privately to your VPC to support AWS services, and it starts without any need of internet gateway or any other resource. So the traffic between VPC and services are not traversed through the internet because in VPC instances don't need the public IP address.

223. **A** (AWS CloudFormation)
Explanation:

To create and manage a set of AWS resources you can use AWS CloudFormation. You can also use it for provisioning and updating them in an orderly fashion, and it is also used to create own templates.

224. **B** (Single Amazon S3 bucket)
Explanation:
The highly available and durable storage is Amazon S3 for given scenario.

225. **D** (Amazon Kinesis)
Explanation:
For processing real-time streaming data Amazon Kinesis is the best cost-effective choice, it helps you to respond immediately to new information rather than waiting for data to be collected before processing starts.

226. **B** (Create CloudFront signed URLs and then distribute these URLs to the users)
Explanation:
With the help of CloudFront, you can securely serve the private data to selected users.

  ✓ By using special CloudFront signed URLs or signed cookies.
  ✓ Your users access Amazon S3 content by using CloudFront URLs; they don't need Amazon S3 URLs. Instead of bypassing the restriction define in Signed URL we recommend you to use CloudFront URLs.

227. **A** (Use AWS OpsWork to define the different layer for your application)
Explanation:
With the help of AWS OpsWorks Stacks, you develop your application as a stack with different data layers because of this you can manage on-premises and AWS applications and servers.

228. **C** (Use IAM policies to create different policies for different t type of users)
Explanation:
With IAM permission you can manage control access to API gateway

  ✓ For deploying API, you grant permission to API developer to perform specific actions.
  ✓ For calling deployed API, you grant permission to API caller to act.

229. **D** (Deploy in 5 AZ with an auto-scaling minimum set to handle a 25% load per zone)
Explanation:
A and B are not appropriate because ELB is not possible for regions. In option D if any AZ goes down application maintain its 100 % availability.

230. **D** (VM import/export)
Explanation:
With the help of VM Import/Export, you can create Amazon Ec2 instances by importing images of VM, or you can export EC2 instance to create VMs.

231. **D** (Use Route53 Health Checks and then do a failover)
Explanation:
Multiple resources that perform the same function then configure DNS failover to route53, so it shifts your traffic from unhealthy resources to healthy resources. With the help of Route53, you can also route traffic to another web server as well.

232. **B** (Enable Server-side encryption on the S3 bucket)
Explanation:
Server-side encryption means you encrypt your data at rest. Which means when you write data in a disk, Amazon S3 will encrypt it and when you access it will decrypt.

233. **C** (Gateway-Cached Volume with snapshots scheduled to Amazon S3)
Explanation:
Gateway-cached volume is best because it gives frequent access to data with low latency although Amazon S3 is the primary storage. Create storage volumes and attach them as iSCSI devices from on-premises application servers then the data written in volume gateway stores it in Amazon S3 and keeping recent read data in on-premises storage gateway cache.

234. **C** (Setup database in a private subnet which connects to the internet via a NAT instance)
Explanation:
If you want web application, which is used publically while core server is not accessible publically, then you need to put a web server in public subnet, and database server in private subnet and communication between both servers can be defined through routing and security.

235. **C** (Create DynamoDB table with required Read and Write capacity and use it as a data layer)
Explanation:
In a given condition, each data size is 30 KB, and DynamoDB is best data layer to store user preferences and it also highly scalable and available service in AWS.

236. **D** (Create Read Replica for the database)
Explanation:
In case of disaster recovery, you can create an Amazon Aurora MySQL DB cluster as a Read Replica in a different AWS Region in this way you can make your data available in another region which is closest to the user.

237. **A** (Consider Using AWS EFS)
Explanation:
Amazon EFS can be used as a standard file system interface and to access the file system. Amazon EFS consolidate with existing application and tools. It can also be used as a common data source for multiple EC2 instances.

238. **C** (Consider moving database server in private subnet)
Explanation:
To enhance security, you need to create an architecture in which database server is in private subnet, and the web server is on a public subnet so it can be accessed by the users over the internet.

239. **A** (SQS helps to facilitate horizontal scaling of encoding tasks)
Explanation:
The reason for using SQS is it helps in the horizontal scaling of AWS resources, or it also guarantees ordering of messages. SQS cannot perform monitoring of health checks and output for transcoding.

240. **C** (Create EBS snapshots and copy them to the destination region) **and D** (Create AMIs for underlying instances)
Explanation:
You can copy an AMI which is used to create a snapshot or template of the instance to another region, or you can make snapshots of the volumes and copy them to the destination region.

241. **D** (Create VPN connection between the on-premises and AWS environment)
Explanation:
For communicating between both environments over the internet, you need to create a VPN connection because it uses IPSecurity to create a secure network.

242. **A** (Consider using Reserved instances for Redshift Cluster)
Explanation:
If you want to run Redshift cluster continuously for a long period, then you must use reserved node because they have reserve compute nodes and you can pay for these reserved node fo particular duration.

243. **C** (AWS Redshift)
Explanation:
To scale you petabyte data storage into AWS you can use Amazon Redshift. In the start, you need data in gigabits and scale it to petabyte or more.

244. **A** (Add an auto scaling group to the setup)
Explanation:
For automatic scaling of AWS resources, in applications, you need to use AWS Auto Scaling by configuring scaling policies.

245. **C** (Use ElastiCache in front of Database)
Explanation:
Amazon ElastiCache is best in-memory caching to cache common read requests.

246. **A** (Consider not using Multi-AZ RDS for implementation database)
Explanation:
Multi-AZ database is suitable for production environment rather than a development environment. Multi-AZ Amazon RDS enhance availability and durability of the database by creating the replica of primary DB instance automatically in different AZ.

247. **B** (Use Amazon S3 to store data) **and C** (Use DynamoDB to store data in tables)
Explanation:

AWS DynamoDB and AWS S3 both are serverless services and no need to maintain servers, so administrative overhead is less, and in this way, your application is highly available.

248. **D** (Use two SQS one with default priority and other is with high priority. So instances poll first high priority than the default priority)
Explanation:
According to the given scenario, you can choose two SQS queues so in this way each queue polled separately and high priority queue will poll first.

249. **B** (The public IP address has changed after the instance was stopped and started)
Explanation:
When instance was stopped and started its configured Public IP address is changed that's why instance public IP address configured to the domain name become invalid.

250. **C** (Amazon SQS)
Explanation:
Amazon SQS is reliable and highly scalable to host queue for storing messages. It is used to decouple systems. It stores request to process audio to be picked up by worker processes.

251. **A** (Amazon EBS general purpose SSD)
Explanation:
As defined that database is not used throughout the day and most cost-effective data type would be EBS general purpose SSD over EBS provisioned IOPS SSD because the minimum volume of throughput optimized HDD is 500 GB, and in the defined scenario, it is 200 GB so for that EBS general purpose SSD is the best choice.

252. **C** (Amazon EFS)
Explanation:
Amazon EFS provides scalable file storage with EC2 instance. It can also be used as a common data source for applications running on multiple instances

253. **D** (Amazon S3 standard infrequent access)
Explanation:

Amazon S3 standard infrequent access is most cost-effective storage for storing data that are not frequently accessed

254. **A** (Expedited retrieval)
Explanation:
Accessing data within 1-5 minutes with $0.03 per GB retrieved is the quality of Expedited retrieval because other features are cost-effective but retrieval time is more than 3 hour.

255. **D** (Attach an internet gateway and add routes for 0.0.0.0/0)
Explanation:
An internet gateway is highly available, redundant and horizontally scalable VPC component and it has no bandwidth restriction on your traffic.

256. **C** (Modify the Cloud Watch Alarm period that provokes auto-scaling scale down policy)
   D (Modify auto scaling group cooldown timers)
Explanation:
Effect of auto-scaling and stabilizing the infrastructure after auto-scaling is taken care by rising the auto scaling group cooldown timer and you can also define a threshold for cloud watch alarm for trigging the scale down policy.

257. **B** (Create DB server security group that allows HTTP port 80 inbound and specify source like a web server security group)
   D (Create a web server security group that allows HTTPs port 443 inbound traffic from anywhere (0.0.0.0/0) and apply it to web servers)
Explanation:
The traffic flow in your web server can be from anywhere by allowing inbound security at 443 and traffic flow from DB server to the web server via database security group.

258. **C** (Prefix each object name with random strings)
Explanation:
When request rate is high then object are stored in the form of portions, and you can use random strings to prefix the object name so distribution is better and performance is also increased.

259.   **C** (Assign IAM roles to the EC2 instance)
        Explanation:
        Roles are used to assigning access to users, application, and services that are not able to access your AWS resources.

260.   **A** (Cache static content using CloudFront)
        Explanation:
        Amazon cloud front is a service which speeds up the distribution of web content and image files to users. It forwards the data throughout the worldwide network of data center called edge locations. When a user request for data which is serving through cloud front then the user is moved toward edge location and provide content with low latency and better performance and if data already in the edge location then it delivers immediately.

261.   **B** (Amazon S3)
        Explanation:
        Lifecycle configuration enables lifecycle management of an object in a bucket. Configuration consist of rules and each rule has actions for Amazon S3 to apply to a group of the object.
        Action #1 is transit action in which you define transition of an object into other storage class.
        Action #2 is expiration action in which you define when the object is expired, and then Amazon S3 deletes that object on your behalf.

262.   **A** (AWS CloudFormation)
        Explanation:
        AWS Cloud Formation helps to use architecture diagram for creating cloud formation template and helps to model and setup AWS resources, so you focus only on your application running and give less time on managing AWS resources because AWS cloud formation is responsible for providing and configuring AWS resources.

263.   **C** (AWS KMS API)
        Explanation:
        AWS KMS is a service which is used to create and control to encryption keys used to encrypt data.

264.   **C** (Take regular EBS snapshots)

Explanation:

You can back up your data by taking a point in time snapshot and save it into Amazon s3. To create new EBS volume, for restoring your data snapshots contain all important information for that.

265.   **A** (Create and configure an Amazon S3 VPC endpoint)
          C (Enable Amazon Redshift Enhanced VPC routing)
        Explanation:
        Amazon Redshift Enhanced VPC routing provides access to Redshift on VPC resources. Redshift needs to enable enhanced VPC routing to access S3 VPC endpoints. In the given scenario, both steps are required to perform.

266.   **C** (Use hexadecimal hash for prefix)
        Explanation:
        In case of high request rate, we need to create randomness to key name for better performance for which hexadecimal hash as a prefix is strongly recommended.

267.   **B** (AWS EFS)
        Explanation:
        For file system storage you can use Amazon Elastic File System (Amazon EFS) with Amazon EC2 instance in AWS Cloud services. With the help of EFS, you can quickly create a file system with high availability and durability over multiple AZ.

268.   **D** (AWS SQS FIFO)
        Explanation:
        AWS SQS FIFO is the service which is used because it's highly scalable and reliable managed message queue service with high throughput and support ordering and at least once processing.

269.   **C** (Amazon ElastiCache)
        Explanation:
        For JSON format data storage Amazon DynamoDB is perfect because it is no SQL database service and provide fast performance with consistent scalability.

270.   **D** (Based on query string parameter)
        Explanation:

As shown in, e.g., that language is defined in the query string parameter, so the configuration in CloudFront is the same.

271. **A** (Amazon SNS
Explanation:
Amazon SNS is used to send text messages or to send messages to enabled devices. With the help of SNS, you can send messages to multiple mobile numbers at once when that number is subscribed to the topic or send directly.

272. **C** (IAM roles for the task)
Explanation:
In a task, IAM roles can be defined that how to be used by the containers. With AWS credentials you can sign in to AWS API request, and manage credential used for the application.

273. **B** (Amazon Redshift)
Explanation:
Amazon Redshift is fully managed and petabyte-scale data storage service in AWS. Column storage for datasets is an essential factor for optimizing analytic query performance in this way as it reduces the load on your disk.

274. **B** (DynamoDB)
     C (ElastiCache)
Explanation:
ElastiCache is a service of AWS which helps to easily set up, manage and scale a distributed in-memory data store or cache environment in the cloud. It provides a cost-effective caching solution.
Amazon DynamoDB is a nonrelational database that delivers reliable performance at any scale. It's a fully managed, multi-region, multi-master database that provides very less latency, and offers built-in security, backup and restore, and in-memory caching.

275. **A** (Store data in S3 bucket and enable versioning.)
Explanation:
Versioning in S3 is at bucket level and can be used to recover a prior version of the object. You can easily recover unintended user actions and application failures both through versioning.

276. **C** (Amazon Aurora)
Explanation:
According to given requirement best storage is Amazon Aurora who has a limit of 64TB storage and easily accommodates the initial 8TB along with the growth of 5GB per day for the longer period, and it has 15 aurora replicas that distributed across Availability zone in a DB cluster.

277. **D** (EBS provisioned IOPS SSD)
Explanation:
For high performance, higher throughput workload and high IOPS requirements provisioned IOPS SSD is the best choice because it supports more than 10000 IOPS or 160 MiB/s of throughput per volume.

278. **D** (Configure lifecycle rule on S3 bucket)
Explanation:
Lifecycle configuration enables lifecycle management of an object in a bucket. Configuration consist of rules and each rule has actions for Amazon S3 to apply to a group of the object.
Action #1 is transit action in which you define transition of an object into other storage class.
Action #2 is expiration action in which you define when the object is expired, and then Amazon S3 deletes that object on your behalf.

279. **C** (AWS EC2)
　　　D (AWS Elastic Beanstalk)
Explanation:
NGINX is an open source for web hosting, caching, load balancing, etc. It complements Amazon ELB by adding support for multiple HTTP, HTTP/2, SSL/TLS services, and many other services.
It will be hosted on an EC2 instance as well as installed in Elastic Bean Stalk.

280. **C** (VPC flow logs)
Explanation:
VPC flow logs can take information of traffic which are going between network interfaces in VPC and store these logs by using Amazon CloudWatch Logs. After storing you can recover that log form Amazon CloudWatch Logs

281. **A** (AWS Aurora)
Explanation:
<u>Amazon Aurora</u> is a MySQL-compatible database. Amazon Aurora has automatically detected database that crashes and restarts without any need for crash recovery. If an entire instance fails amazon aurora will automatically failover to one of up to 15 read replicas.

282. **C** (Enable cross region snapshots for Redshift cluster)
Explanation:
Enable snapshot of cross-region that is available for Redshift cluster to make it available in different regions.

283. **B** (Use AWS KMS customer master key)
Explanation:
To encrypt database Amazon Redshift uses encryption keys and to manage these hierarchy keys you can use AWS Key Management Service (AWS KMS) or a hardware security module (HSM). Depending upon the management of these keys the process of encryption changes.

284. **D** (AWS EBS volumes)
Explanation:
An Amazon EBS volume is block-level storage which can be attached to a single EC2 instance. It is also used as primary storage.

285. **D** (EBS Throughput Optimized)
Explanation:
For such type of storage volume in which batch processing activity is done with larger throughput at low cost then we will go with EBS throughput optimized.

286. **C** (Amazon S3)
Explanation:
Amazon S3 storage is used for these requirements because it has the capability of versioning and best storage for storing documents and any object. Versioning is at bucket level and can recover the previous version of the object. Versioning is the

process in which when the object is store it will store in Amazon S3 bucket with version ID, and this will be the current version of the object. When you again store the object, it will store with another unique version id which is the version id of the object, and the previous object is store behind that new object in this way when you delete object it will delete new version id object, and last version id become the current version of the object.

287. **A** (2 EC2 Instances in us-east-2a, 2 EC2 Instances in us-east-2b and 2 EC2 Instances in us-east-2c)

   C (4 EC2 Instances in us-east-2a, 4 EC2 Instance in us-east-2b and no EC2 Instances in us-east-2c)

   Explanation:

   Option a and c is correct. Because if any of the availability zones is unavailable, you always have 4 EC2 instances available.

288. **C** (Store file in S3 bucket and use Amazon S3 event notification to request a lambda function for processing)

   Explanation:

   You can create first lambda function to process the file with code then request to lambda function through event notification in S3 bucket for processing.

289. **B** (Amazon Aurora)

   Explanation:

   Amazon Aurora is the RDS engine which meets the above requirement because it can grow up to 64TB in size with a replica delay of fewer than 100 milliseconds. Amazon Aurora is fully manageable, MySQL and PostgreSQL compatible DB. It delivers up to 5 times the throughput of MySQL without any changing in the application.

290. **B** (AWS Elastic Beanstalk)

   Explanation:

   Elastic Beanstalk is the service used in solution architecture for workloads like creating a web application using Amazon RDS and long-running worker process

because ELB provides AWS resource to run an application in web application and ELB in worker environment it provides support files for programming languages and a daemon on EC2 instance.

291. **B** (Use VPC peering between both accounts)
Explanation:
Two VPC's can communicate to each other or any instance in any of the VPC connect to another in the same network with the use of VPC peering connection because it is a networking connection.

292. **D** (Migrate NAT instance to a NAT gateway and host it in public subnet)
Explanation:
By the help of using deployed NAT instance, you can start or stop using NAT gateway, but NAT gateway must be deployed in public subnet.

293. **B** (NAT Instance)
Explanation:
For high availability launching of NAT instance in multiple AZ is an important part of the architecture and make it as a part of auto scaling group.

294. **A** (Using API gateway along with AWS Lambda)
Explanation:
Since they have ownership of API, so the best choice is to convert the code for API and use it in a lambda function. In this way, you save your cost because you must pay only for the time to function because lambda gives high availability and scalability to your code.

295. **C** (EBS provisioned IOPS)
Explanation:
For high performance with high IOPS, EBS provisioned IOPS SSD is the best choice. For high performance, higher throughput workload and high IOPS requirements provisioned IOPS SSD is the best choice because it supports more than 10000 IOPS or 160 MiB/s of throughput per volume.

296.   **A** (Amazon DynamoDB)
       Explanation:
       The most efficient storage to store metadata is AWS DynamoDB. It is used along with Amazon S3, or you can create secondary indexes for DynamoDB tables.

297.   **A** (Create a snapshot and copy it in another region)
       Explanation:
       Snapshot is like backup; when you create snapshots of EBS volumes, then you can use these snapshots for creating a new volume in the same region or by copying it across the region so you can use it in multiple regions.

298.   **D** (Configured dynamic scaling and use target tracking scaling group)
       Explanation:
       Target tracking scaling policies simplify how you configure dynamic scaling. You select a predefined metric or configure a customized metric then set target value. If your scaling is based on a metric which is utilization and it increases or decreases proportionally to some instances in auto scaling group.

299.   **C** (Use cloud trail to monitor the API activity)
       D (Use Cloud Watch metrics for the metrics that need to be monitored as per requirement and set up an activity to send out a notification when metric reaches the set threshold limit)
       Explanation:
       To monitor AWS API calls, AWS Cloud trial is a service, it keeps a record of API gateway and forwards the logs to S3 bucket. AWS CloudWatch metric is also used to monitor metrics.

300.   **D** (Ensure that CloudTrail trail is enabled for all region)
       Explanation:
       AWS cloud trial is used to record user action by the history of AWS API calls from your account.

Creating trial with default setting on AWS Cloud trial console by creating it in all region with a recording of log in each region and delivery of logs file to Amazon S3 bucket. You can also enable Simple notification service (SNS) for notification of logs delivery.

301. **C** (Configured Storage Gateway Stored Volume)
Explanation:
iSCSI target is provided in volume gateway. In stored volume, your primary data is stored locally with the availability of entire data set for low latency frequently accessed. In stored volume data is also backup asynchronously by taking on-time snapshots to S3.

302. **B** (VPC endpoint)
Explanation:
A VPC endpoint connects you privately to your VPC to support AWS services, and it starts without any need of internet gateway or any other resource. So the traffic between VPC and services are not traversed through the internet because in VPC instances don't need the public IP address.

303. **A** (Use auto-scaling for backend instances)
     C (Use auto-scaling for proxy servers)
Explanation:
In case of scaling always consider autoscaling service of AWS. It can scale both the proxy server and a backend instance.

304. **C** (Use Route53 to route to the static website)
Explanation:
In case of any disaster, the best choice of recovery scenario is to move traffic to a static website because in disaster scenario we assume that entire region is affected, so we need service to be provided form another region. But ELB cannot span across regions.

305. **B** (Enter the NS record from Route53 in domain registrar)
     D (Use Route53 with the static website in S3)
Explanation:

A static website is hosted in S3, but you need to enter the nameserver records for Route53 in domain registrar.

306.   **B** (Set up an ElastiCache in front of a database)
   Explanation:
   If we use ElastiCache in front of the database, then it caches common queries, and in this way, the load on the database is reduced.

307.   **C** (Use Multi-AZ for the RDS instance to ensure that a secondary database is created in another AZ)
   Explanation:
   Multi-AZ Amazon RDS helps to improve the availability of DB by automatically creating primary DB instance and its replica to standby instance in another AZ.

308.   **A** (Use public subnet for the web tier and a private subnet for the database layer)
   Explanation:
   The ideal setup in VPC is that to host the web server on a public subnet so that the users on the internet can access it. The data server can be hosted on a private subnet.

309.   **D** (Push web clicks by session to amazon kinesis and analyze behavior using kinesis workers)
   Explanation:
   To continuously capture and analyze the data streams you can use Amazon Kinesis data streams.

310.   **C** (Use Kinesis Firehose with S3 to take logs and store them in S3 for further processing)
   Explanation:
   To capture, transform and store streaming data into data stores like Amazon S3 for the future stage you can use Amazon Kinesis Data Firehose.

311. **D** (Create a pre-signed URL for each profile which will last for the monthly duration)

Explanation:

With the help of pre-signed URL, you can define which user/customer can upload an object to your bucket by giving temporary access. Initially, all the objects and bucket are private. Pre-signed URL is valid for some specific duration.

312.   **D** (Use ECS for container orchestration and the combination of spot and reserved instances for underlying instance)

Explanation:

You can use elastic container service for container orchestration and for critical and no critical data you can use spot instances and reserved instances for keeping cost minimal.

313. **D** (AWS S3 standard)

Explanation:

As per requirement retrieval time is seven hr. which meets the frame of Amazon glacier cost-effectively.

314.   **B** (Multivalue answer)

Explanation:

Multi-value answer policy is used when you want to use Route53 to respond to the DNS queries with up to eight healthy records randomly because of Route53 response differently to different DNS resolver. In this way when your web server becomes unavailable after response caches, then the client can try other IP address in response.

315.   **C** (AWS Aurora)

Explanation:

According to the given condition best choice is Amazon Aurora. Amazon Aurora is the RDS engine which meets the above requirement because it can grow up to 64TB in size with a replica delay of fewer than 100 milliseconds. Amazon Aurora is fully manageable, MySQL and PostgreSQL compatible DB. It delivers up to 5 times the throughput of MySQL without any changing in the application.

316. **D** (Use AWS Kinesis streams to process and analyze data)
Explanation:
For storing, processing and analyzing real-time streaming Amazon Kinesis can be used.

317. **C** (AWS Redshift)
Explanation:
For the given condition, ideal storage is Amazon Redshift which is helpful to scale your data storage in the cloud by starting initially with gigabytes of data and scale up to a petabyte. With the help of Amazon Redshift, you can perform fast analyzing of the query by uploading files on a cluster of Redshift.

318. **A** (Use KMS to generate encryption keys which can be used to encrypt the volume)
Explanation:
You can encrypt volume when you create volume with the help of keys generated by Key management service.

319. **A** (Use AWS Lambda to store a change record in DynamoDB table)
     C (Use Cloudwatch events to monitor the state changes of the event)
Explanation:
Cloud watch event used to monitor a state change of event and with the help of AWS lambda store the change record in DynamoDB table.

320. **A** (Use NAT gateway to allow the instances in the private subnet to download the updates)
Explanation:
To download updates from the internet in instances which is in private subnet you need NAT gateway.

321. **C** (Cold HDD)
Explanation:

The most cost-efficient storage type is Cold HDD. It is for less frequently access data.

322.   **D** (Use Amazon S3 to host the files)
Explanation:
With the help of Amazon S3, you can use public URL for future downloading because when you upload a file, it gets automatically Public URL.

323.   **A** (Create a database security group and ensure that the web server's security group allows incoming access)
       C (Place the EC2 instances with Oracle database in a separate private subnet)
Explanation:
Secure way is to place the database in private subnet and ensure that access only allowed from web servers.

324.   **C** (Use IAM roles with right permission to interact with DynamoDB and assign it to EC2 instance)
Explanation:
Always assign IAM roles to EC2 instance to access AWS resources or DynamoDB. It also defines permission policies to identity in AWS about what they can or cannot access.

325.   **C** (AWS ElastiCache)
Explanation:
ElastiCache is a service of AWS which helps to easily set up, manage and scale a distributed in-memory data store or cache environment in the cloud. It provides a cost-effective caching solution. With the help of ElastiCache, you can improve the performance of an application by retrieving data with low latency.

326.   **A** (Trigger a Lambda function to create an associated entry in the application as soon as DynamoDB streams are modified
       D (Use DynamoDB streams to track the changes to DynamoDB table)
Explanation:

When DynamoDB streams set up on a table, you can associate the stream ARN with Lambda function that you write. When an item modified in the table, a new record appears in table stream then AWS Lambda polls the stream and request Lambda function synchronously when it detects new stream records. And according to our given condition, we need immediate entry to an application, and AWS lambda function also required when there is a change in DynamoDB table.

DynamoDB streams can also be used to monitor DynamoDB table.

327.   **C** (Make use of AWS SQS to manage the messages)
        Explanation:
        To manage messages between application components AWS SQS is best to choose, it is highly scalable and durable service.

328.   **A** (Make use of Read replicas to set up a secondary read-only database)
        Explanation:
        For heavy read database workload, Amazon RDS Read Replicas gives the capability to scale single DB instance. By creating one or more replicas of primary DB, you can serve the application for high read traffic through multiple copies.

329.   **C** (Use S3 lifecycle policy to manage the deletion)
        Explanation:
        Lifecycle configuration enables lifecycle management of an object in a bucket. Configuration consist of rules and each rule has actions for Amazon S3 to apply to a group of the object.
        Action #1 is transit action in which you define transition of an object into other storage class.
        Action #2 is expiration action in which you define when the object is expired, and then Amazon S3 deletes that object on your behalf.

330.   **C** (Access data through a VPC endpoint for Amazon S3)
        Explanation:
        A VPC endpoint connects you privately to your VPC to support AWS services, and it starts without any need of internet gateway or any other resource. So the traffic

between VPC and services are not traversed through the internet because in VPC instances don't need the public IP address. Traffic between your VPC and the other service does not leave the Amazon network.

331. **D** (Change the security group for the cluster)
Explanation:
By default, Amazon Redshift Cluster is not accessible when you set up. So, you need to link the cluster with security group to allow users inbound access.

332. **B** (Place EC2 instance behind CloudFront)
Explanation:
Amazon CloudFront is a web service which delivers the content through edge locations and when a user request for the content which serves through CloudFront will route toward CloudFront and provide content with low latency.

333. **D** (Create NAT gateway in another availability zone)
Explanation:
You need to create NAT gateway in each AZ so the resource in that AZ will use their NAT gateway. In this way, you make NAT gateway highly available because if resources in multiple AZ use single NAT gateway and when NAT gateway AZ goes down then resources in other AZ will lose internet access.

334. **B** (AWS Aurora)
Explanation:
Amazon Aurora is fully manageable, MySQL and PostgreSQL compatible DB. It delivers up to 5 times the throughput of MySQL without any changing in the application.

335. **A** (Public subnets for the application tier and NAT gateway, and private subnets for the database cluster)
Explanation:

You need to create NAT gateway in public subnet then update route table to link it with private subnets to point incoming internet traffic to NAT gateway in this way private subnet instances communicate over the internet.

336. **D** (Use pre-signed URLs instead to upload an image)
      Explanation:
      With the help of Pre-signed URL, you can upload an image to S3. With the help of pre-signed URL, you can define which user/customer can upload an object to your bucket. Initially, all the objects and bucket are private. They are valid for some specific duration.

337. **D** (EBS provisioned IOPS)
      Explanation:
      For this scenario, ideal storage is provisioned IOPS SSD. For high performance, higher throughput workload and high IOPS requirements provisioned IOPS SSD is the best choice because it supports more than 10000 IOPS or 160 MiB/s of throughput per volume.

338. **C** (Use Route53 health checks to monitor the endpoints)
      Explanation:
      For monitoring endpoints, the ideal choice is Route53 health checks that can access the endpoints via the internet and then monitor it at regular intervals. The endpoint is defined by domain name or IP address.

339. **A** (Upload logs to Amazon Kinesis and then analyze logs accordingly)
      Explanation:
      For storing, processing and analyzing real-time streaming Amazon Kinesis can be used.

340. **D** (Add auto scaling group
      Explanation:
      To increase cumulative system availability, you need to balance the resources across multiple AZ by configuring multiple zones in auto scaling group setting.

341.   **D** (AWS DynamoDB)
       Explanation:
       For durable storage of metadata, Amazon DynamoDB is best to choose.

342.   **D** (Use Elastic Beanstalk to provision the environment quickly)
       Explanation:
       Elastic Beanstalk is the quickest way to deploy your application in AWS independent of worrying about infrastructure. You upload application, and Elastic Beanstalk handles the capacity provision, health check, and other management complexities.

343.   **B** (AWS EFS)
       Explanation:
       For file system storage you can use Amazon Elastic File System (Amazon EFS) with Amazon EC2 instance in AWS Cloud services. With the help of EFS, you can quickly create a file system with high availability and durability over multiple AZ.

344.   **D** (Amazon S3 standard infrequent access)
       Explanation:
       Amazon S3 infrequent access is perfect for storing less frequent access data. It is the most cost-effective storage.

345.   **D**(Attach an internet gateway and add routes for 0.0.0.0/0)
       Explanation:
       An internet gateway is highly available, redundant and horizontally scalable VPC component and it has no bandwidth restriction on your traffic. It allows communication between instances and the internet.

346.   **B** (Ensure that the right metrics are being used to trigger the scale out)
       Explanation:
       If you want to scale as much as you want you to need to perform scaling events on right metrics and must have to define a right threshold.

347.   **C** (Prefix each object name with random strings)
       Explanation:

When request rate is high then object are stored in the form of portions, and you can use random strings to prefix the object name so distribution is better and performance is also increased.

348. **D** (AWS CloudFormation)
Explanation:
AWS CloudFormation helps to create code templates for providing resources to build and rebuild infrastructure without any manual action. Cloud formation takes care of determining the right operations to perform when managing your stack and the rollback changes automatically if errors are detected.

349. **C** (Use EBS snapshots to create volumes in another region)
Explanation:
Snapshot is like backup; when you create snapshots of EBS volumes, then you can use these snapshots for creating a new volume in the same region or by copying it across the region so you can use it in multiple regions in case of disaster.

350. **B** (Enable VPC Flow logs)
  C (Capture requests which are sent to the CloudFront API)
Explanation:
In case of PCI and HIPAA complaint workloads, you need to log your CloudFront usage data by enabling CloudFront access logs or capture requests that are sent to the CloudFront API for future auditing purpose.

351. **A** (Use SNS service to send notification)
Explanation:
AWS SNS is a web service that manages the delivery of messages to subscribing clients.

352. **B** (Use AMIs to recreate the EC2 instances in another region)
Explanation:
With the help of AMI, you can create an instance in another region by simply copying it in another region.

353.   **C** (Enable Amazon Redshift enhanced VPC routing)
Explanation:
By enabling Enhanced VPC Routing in Amazon Redshift, the traffic between data repositories and the cluster will go through VPC rather than the internet.

354.   **D** (Use the VM import tools)
Explanation:
VM Import/Export tool enables you to easily import virtual machine images from your existing environment to Amazon EC2 instances and export them back to your on-premises environment.

355.   **C** (AWS EBS)
Explanation:
An Amazon EBS volume is block-level storage which can be attached to a single EC2 instance. EBS is highly available and reliable storage.

356.   **D** (Use AWS Lambda function with C# for IT jobs)
Explanation:
The most efficient way to host jobs by using AWS Lambda because this can run code in C# programming language.

357.   **B** (Use the AWS cloud trail to monitor all API activity)
Explanation:
AWS CloudTrail is a service to continuously monitor and logs the account activity across your infrastructure and Amazon CloudWatch logs are used to monitor, store and access logs file from EC2 instances and other sources.

358.   **B** (AWS Aurora)
         D (AWS Redshift)
Explanation:
Amazon Redshift is fully managed and petabyte-scale data storage service in AWS. Column storage for datasets is an essential factor for optimizing analytic query performance in this way as it reduces the load on your disk.

Amazon Aurora is fully manageable, MySQL and PostgreSQL compatible DB. By applying multi-master in Amazon Aurora, you can operate heavy read/write workloads with higher availability.

359. **C** (Ensure that unnecessary manual snapshots of the cluster are deleted)
Explanation:
For snapshots in Amazon Redshift, there is free storage which is equal to the storage capacity of the cluster. You can manage snapshots automatically for a specific duration and delete snapshots manually which you don't need.

360. **A** (Use VPC peering to peer both VPCs)
Explanation:
Two VPC's can communicate to each other or any instance in any of the VPC connect to another in the same network with the use of VPC peering connection because it is a networking connection.

361. **B** (Add more instances in existing availability zone)
     D (Add an auto scaling group to setup)
Explanation:
By using Amazon EC2 auto-scaling, you can gain benefits of AWS like fault tolerance and better availability. By using Amazon Ec2 autoscaling you can replace the instances which are unhealthy, and you can handle the massive amount of traffic.

362. **B** (Organization start using Gateway-Cached Volumes)
Explanation:
According to given scenario they want extra storage, not backup, so for this purpose gateway-cached volume is best in this way organization don't need scaling of their on-premises infrastructure, and they store in AWS storage service while having the most recent file available at low latency.

363. **D** (Store data in S3 bucket and enable versioning)
Explanation:
Amazon S3 storage is used for these requirements because it has the capability of versioning and best storage for storing documents and any object. Versioning is at bucket level and can recover the previous version of the object. Versioning is the

process in which when the object is store it will store in Amazon S3 bucket with version ID, and this will be the current version of the object. When you again store the object, it will store with another unique version id, which is the version id of the object, and the previous object is store behind that new object in this way when you delete object it will delete new version id object, and previous version id become the current version of the object.

364. **D** (Amazon Aurora)
Explanation:
According to given requirement best storage is Amazon Aurora who has a limit of 64TB storage and easily accommodates the initial 5TB along with the growth of 7GB per day for the longer period, and it has 15 aurora replicas that distributed across Availability zone in a DB cluster.

365. **B** (Place S3 bucket behind the CloudFront distribution)
Explanation:
You can use Amazon CloudFront with Amazon S3 because CloudFront performs distribution of content with high data transfer rate and low latency in this way you can optimize response to all customers.

366. **C** (AWS SQS FIFO)
Explanation:
AWS SQS FIFO is the service which is used because it's highly scalable and reliable managed message queue service with high throughput and support ordering and at least once processing. Duplicating of the message will not occur also.

367. **B** (AWS S3)
Explanation:
AWS Lambda is a service which is stateless mean it doesn't require any last interactions and no need to store session data and can scale horizontally.

368. **C** (Use an AWS load balancer to distribute the traffic)
      D (Ensure instances are placed in separate regions)
Explanation:

An ELB can be used to distribute the traffic among multiple instances in multiple AZ. An ELB automatically detects faulty instance and then route the traffic to other instance. In this way, it increases fault tolerance.

369. **A** (Use spot instances for underlying EC2 instance)
Explanation:
If you are not worried about your application whether it starts or resume operations, you can use Spot Instances. It is also a cost-effective solution.

370. **B** (Load data in Amazon Elastic Search)
   D (Use an AWS lambda function which gets triggered whenever data is added to the S3 bucket)
Explanation:
You can use AWS elastic search with Amazon S3 because ES can have the searching capability. When you link ES with Amazon S3 and AWS Lambda, an event notification trigger to AWS Lambda whenever the data send to S3.

371. **A** (Deploy image as an Amazon ECS task)

   D (Create Docker image of your batch processing application)
Explanation:
For batch processing workload you can use Docker containers. You need to create docker image so you can copy it wherever you want like ECS task.

372. **B** (Create DB server security group that allows MySQL port 3306 inbound and specify source like a web server security group)
   D (d. Create a web server security group that allows HTTPs port 443 inbound traffic from anywhere (0.0.0.0/0) and apply it to web servers)
Explanation:
The traffic flow in your web server can be from anywhere by allowing inbound security at 443 and traffic flow from DB server to the web server via database security group.

373. **C** (Configure failover routing policy)
Explanation:

Failover routing policy is used to configure active-passive failover in which you need to create separate primary and secondary failover record with health checks.

374. **D** (Use cloud formation templates to provision the resources accordingly)
Explanation:
To create and manage a set of AWS resources you can use AWS CloudFormation. You can also use it for provisioning and updating them in an orderly fashion, and it is also used to create own templates for a short-lived environment like test environment.

375. **C** (Create an EC2 instance and install database service accordingly)
Explanation:
For self-managed database you need an EC2instance then you have complete control over the underlying database.

376. **B** (Amazon Aurora)
Explanation:
Amazon Aurora is the RDS engine which meets the above requirement because it can grow up to 64TB in size with a replica delay of fewer than 100 milliseconds. Amazon Aurora is fully manageable, MySQL and PostgreSQL compatible DB. It delivers up to 5 times the throughput of MySQL without any changing in the application.

377. **D** (Direct connection)
Explanation:
For a dedicated connection, you can use AWS Direct Connect in AWS. It helps to create secure and private connectivity with consistency between your on-premises data centers and AWS.

378. **B** (AWS Glacier)
Explanation:
According to the given condition, Amazon Glacier is the best choice for long-term back up at low cost and retrieval time is from a few minutes to 12 hours depending upon the size of data.

379. **D** (Elastic load balancing, Amazon EC2 instance, and autoscaling)
Explanation:
For scalable and elastic web tier we need autoscaling process to increase or decrease the number of EC2 instances according to requirement with an elastic load balancer.

380. **A** (Outbound network ACL needs to be configured to allow outbound traffic)
Explanation:
To allow SSH on EC2 instance, you need to configure Network ACL allow to both inbound and outbound traffic because network ACL are stateless. So responses to allowed inbound traffic are subjected to rules for outbound traffic (and vice versa). In the security group response is stateful so if the incoming request is granted by default outbound request is also allowed.

381. B) Amazon S3

Explanation

Amazon s3 is a perfect storage layer for storing documents and other types of object

382. c) Enable Multi-AZ for the AWS RDS Database

Explanation

Amazon RDS Multi AZ deployments give enhanced availability and durability for Database instance, making them a natural right for production database workloads. When you provision a Multi AZ database Instance, Amazon RDs automatically makes a first DB Instance and synchronously replicates the information to a standby instance in a different Availability Zone. Each AZ runs on its private physically distinct, independent infrastructure, and is engineered to be greatly reliable. In case of infrastructure disaster, Amazon RDS performs an automatic failover to the standby, so that you can restart database operations as soon as the failover is done. Since the endpoint for your database instance remains similar after a failover, your application can continue database operation without the requirement for manual administrative intervention.

383. C. Add an event with notification sends to Lambda

D. Create an AWS Lambda function to insert the required entry for each uploaded files
Explanation

You can create a Lambda function containing the code to process the file, and add the name of the file to the DynamoDB table

You can then use an event Notification from the S3 bucket to invoke the Lambda function whenever the file is uploaded

384.

   a)   Amazon Aurora

Explanation

Amazon Aurora is a fully managed, PostgreSQL-Compatible and MySQL-, relational database engine. It joins the speed and reliability of high-end commercial database with the simplicity and cost-effectiveness of open-source database. It delivers up to 5 times the throughput of MySQL and up to three the throughput of PostgreSQL without needing changes to most of your existing applications.

All Aurora Replicas return the equal data for query results with minimal replica lag-usually much lesser than 100 milliseconds after the prime instance has written an update

385.

   a)   Use S3 website hosting to host the website

Explanation

Anyone can host a static website on Amazon (SSS) simple storage service. On a static website, individual webpages include static content. They might also contain client-side scripts

386.

   a) Amazon EBS general purpose SSD

Explanation

This volume type is optimized for workloads involving large, sequential I/O, and we recommend that customer with workloads performing small, random I/O use gp2

For more information, see

https://docs.aws.amazon.com/AWSEC2/latest/UserGuide/EBSVolumeTypes.html#ineffici ency

387.

c)   Amazon EFS

Explanation

Amazon EFS is providing scalable file storage for use with Amazon EC2. You can create an EFS file system and configure your instances to mount the file system. You can use an EFS

file system as a common data source for workloads and applications running on multiple instances.

388.

    b) Create a lifecycle policy to transfer the object to S3-infrequent access storage after a certain duration of time

    c) Store the object in the S3-Standard storage

Explanation

Store the images initially in standard storage since they are accessed frequently. Define lifecycle policies to move the images the images to infrequent access storage to save on cost

Amazon S3 infrequent access is perfect if you want to store data that is not frequently accessed and is must cost-effective than option D

For more information use

https://aws.amazon.com/s3/storage-classes/

389.

    b) Using bulk retrieval

Explanation

Expedited retrievals let you to quickly access your documents when occasional urgent requests for a subset of archives are required

390.

    a)   AWS EKS

Explanation

Amazon Elastic Container Service for Kubernetes is a managed service that makes it easy for you to run Kubernetes on Amazon web services without needing to install and operate your own Kubernetes clusters.

391.

    b)   Increase the auto scaling cooldown timer value

Explanation

The Cooldown period is a configurable setting for your Auto Scaling group which ensures that it doesn't launch or terminate additional instances before the previous scaling activity takes effect. After the Auto Scaling group dynamically scales using a simple Scaling Policy, it waits for the Cooldown time to complete before continuing

392.

    a)   Change the inbound NACL to deny access from the suspect IP

Explanation

A network access control list is an optional layer of security for your VPC that acts as a firewall for controlling traffic flow in and out of one or many subnets. You might set up network ACLs with rules parallel to your security groups to add more layer of security to your VPC.

393.

    a)   Prefix each object name with a random string

Explanation

If the request rate is high, you can use hash keys or random strings to prefix to the object name. Here, partitions used to store the objects will be better distributed and hence allow for better read/write performance for your objects.

394.

    a)   Create and assign an IAM role to the EC2 instance

Explanation

Anyone can use roles to delegate access to clients, applications, or services that don't normally have access to your AWS resources. It is not a good practice to use IAM credentials for a production-based application. It is always a good practice to use IAM Roles.

395.

c)   Use CloudFront with the S3 bucket as the source

Explanation

Amazon CloudFront is a web service that boosts up distribution of static and dynamic web content, such as .css, .html, .js, and image files, to your client. CloudFront delivers your content through a global network of data centers called Edge locations. When a client requests content that you are serving with CloudFront, the client is routed to the Edge location that gives the lowest latency, so that content is provided with the best possible performance.

396.

    b)   Use S3 with standard redundancy to store and serve the scanned files. Use CloudSearch for the query (processing, and use Elastic Beanstalk to host the website across multiple Availability zones)

Explanation

With Amazon CloudSearch, you can rapidly add rich search capabilities to your website or application. You do not want to become a search expert or worry about hardware provisioning, setup, and maintenance. With a few clicks in the Amazon web services Management Console, you can make a search domain and upload the data that you need to make searchable, and Amazon CloudSearch will automatically provision the required resources and deploy an extremely tuned search index.

You can change your search parameters with no trouble, fine tune search relevance, and apply new settings at any period. As your volume of traffic and data fluctuates, Amazon CloudSearch seamlessly scales to meet your requirements.

397.

    c)   Use AWS direct connect

Explanation

Amazon web services Direct Connect makes it easy to establish a dedicated network connection from your premises to Amazon web services. Using Amazon web services Direct Connect, you can establish private connectivity between Amazon web services and your office, datacenter, or colocation environment, which in many cases can decrease your network costs, increase bandwidth throughput, and offer a more consistent network experience than Internet-based connections.

398.

a)   Tag the production instances with a production-identifying tag and add resource-level permissions to the developers with an explicit deny on the terminate API call to instances with the production tag.

b)   Create a separate AWS account and add the developers to that account

Explanation

Creating separate AWS account for developers will help the organization to facilitate the highest level of resource and security isolation.

The following documentation from AWS gives us a clear picture of the scenarios when we need to consider creating multiple accounts.

There is no one-size-fits-all response for how much Amazon web services account particular clients should have, most organizations will want to create more than one Amazon web services account because multiple accounts give the highest level of resource and security isolation. Answering 'yes' to any of the following questions is a good indication that you should consider creating additional Amazon web services accounts.

- Does the business want administrative isolation between workloads? Administrative isolation by account gives the most straightforward approach for granting independent administrative groups dissimilar levels of administrative control over Amazon web services resources based on the workload, development lifecycle, business unit, or data sensitivity.
- Does the business need limited visibility and discoverability of workloads? Accounts offer a natural boundary for visibility and discoverability. Workloads can't be accessed or viewed unless an administrator of the account enables access to client managed in another account.
- Does the business need isolation to minimize the blast radius? Blast-radius isolation by account gives a mechanism for limiting the impact of a critical event such as a security breach if an Amazon web services Region or Availability Zone becomes unapproachable, account suspensions, etc. Separate accounts help define boundaries and give natural blast radius isolation.
- Does the business need strong isolation of recovery and/or auditing data? Businesses that need to control access and visibility to auditing information due to regulatory needs can isolate their recovery information and/or auditing data in an account separate from where they run their workloads.

399.
 a) Amazon SNS
 b) Amazon Cloudwatch

Explanation

Amazon CloudWatch may be used to monitor IOPS metrics from the RDS instance and Amazon Simple Notification Service, to send the notification if any alarm is triggered.

400.

b)   Remove public read access and use signed URLs with expiry dates

Explanation

You can distribute private content consuming a signed (URL) that is valid for only a short time possibly for as little as a few min. Signed (URLs) that are valid for like a short time period are good for distributing content on the fly to a user for a limited purpose, like distributing movie rentals or music downloads to the client on demand.

401.
 c) AWS CloudFormation

Explanation

The AWS Documentation mentions the below on AWS CloudFormation. This supplements the requirement in the question about consultants using their architecture diagrams to construct CloudFormation templates.

Amazon web services CloudFormation is a service that benefits you model and set up your AWS resources so that you can spend less period managing those resources and more period focusing on your applications that run in Amazon web services. You make a template that describes all the Amazon web services resources that you want, and Amazon web services CloudFormation takes care of provisioning and configuring those resources for you.

402.

   a)   AWS KMS

Explanation

Amazon web services Key Management Service is a managed service that makes it easy for you to make and control the encryption keys used to encrypt your data. Amazon web services key management service is integrated with other Amazon web services including Amazon Elastic Block Store, Amazon Simple Storage Service, Amazon Redshift, Amazon Elastic Transcoder, Amazon WorkMail, Amazon Relational Database Service, and others to make it simple to encrypt your data with encryption keys that you manage.

403.

d)   Nothing, since by default, EBS volumes are required within their Availability zone

Explanation

Amazon Elastic Block Store gives persistent block storage volumes for use with Amazon EC2 instances in the Amazon web services Cloud. Each Amazon elastic block storage volume is automatically replicated within its Availability Zone (AZ) to protect you from component failure, durability and offering high availability. Amazon (EBS) volumes offer the consistent and low latency performance required to run your workloads. With Amazon elastic block storage, you can scale your usage up or down within minutes all while paying a little price for only what you provision.

404.

d)   AWS DynamoDB

Explanation

Amazon DynamoDB is a fast and flexible (NoSQL) DB service for all applications that require consistent, single-digit millisecond latency at any scale. It is a fully managed cloud DB and supports both document and key-value store models. Its flexible data model,

automatic scaling, and reliable performance of throughput capacity make it a great fit for mobile, IoT, gaming, ad tech, web, and many other applications.

405.
   a)   AWS SQS

Explanation

Amazon (SQS) is a fully managed message queuing service that makes it easy to decouple and scale microservices, serverless applications, and distributed systems. Building applications from individual components that each achieve a discrete function improve scalability and reliability and is best practice design for modern applications. SQS makes it simple and cost-effective to decouple and coordinate the components of a cloud application. Using SQS, you can send, receive, and store messages between software components at any volume, without losing messages or needing other services to be always available.

406.
   a)   AWS STS

Explanation

You can use the Amazon web services Security Token Service to create and give trusted clients with security credentials that could control access to your Amazon web services resources. Temporary security credentials are short term, as the name implies. They could be configured to last for anywhere from a few min to many hours. After the credentials expire, Amazon web services no longer recognizes them or enable any kind of access from API requests to create with them.

407.
   a)   Use Auto-scaling group

Explanation

AWS Auto Scaling monitors your applications and automatically adjusts capacity to maintain steady, predictable performance at the lowest possible cost. Using AWS Auto Scaling, it is easy to setup application scaling for multiple resources across multiple services in minutes.

408.
   a)   AWS ElastiCache

Explanation

Amazon ElastiCache offers completely managed Redis and Memcached. Seamlessly Operate, deploy, and scale popular open source compatible in-memory data stores. Build

data-intensive apps or improve the performance of your existing apps by retrieving information from huge throughput and short latency in-memory data stores. Amazon ElastiCache is a popular selection for Gaming, Ad-Tech, IoT apps Financial Services, and Healthcare.

409.

 a) EBS provisioned IOPS SSD

Explanation

Provisioned IOPS SSD (io1)

Highest performance SSD volume for mission-critical low latency or high throughput workloads.

410.

 a) AWS Elastic Beanstalk

Explanation

The Elastic Beanstalk is an easy-to-use service for deploying and scaling web applications and services.

We can simply upload code, and Elastic Beanstalk automatically handles the deployment, from capacity provisioning, load balancing, Auto-Scaling, to application health monitoring. Meanwhile, we can retain full control over the AWS resources used in the application and access the underlying resources at any time.

Hence, A is the correct answer

411.

 a) Use IAM permission to control the access

Explanation

You control access to Amazon API gateway with Identity and access management permission by controlling access to the following two API gateway component process.

- To create, deploy, and manage an API in API Gateway, you must allow the API developer permissions to perform the essential actions supported by the API management component of API Gateway.
- To call a deployed API or to refresh the API caching, you must grant the API caller permissions to perform required IAM actions supported by the API execution component of API Gateway.

412.

a)	Establish a VPC peering

Explanation

A VPC peering connection is a connection between 2 VPCs that enables you to route traffic between them privately. Instances in either VPC could communicate with each other as if they are within the same network. You can make a VPC peering connection between your own VPCs, with a VPC in another AWS account, or with a VPC in a different AWS Region.

413.

a)	Choosing Spot instances for the underlying nodes

Explanation

Spot Instances in Amazon EMR provide an option to purchase Amazon EC2 instance capacity at a reduced cost as compared to On-Demand purchasing.

414.

a)	Use pre-signed URLs

Explanation

All objects by default are private. Only the object owner has permission to access these objects. However, the object owner can optionally share objects with others by creating a pre-signed URL, using their own security credentials, to grant time-limited permission to download the objects.

415.

a)	Use dynamoDB streams to monitor the changes in the dynamoDB table

Explanation

A DynamoDB Stream is an ordered flow of information about changes to items in an Amazon DynamoDB table. When you enable a stream on a table, DynamoDB captures information about every modification to data items in the table.

416.

a)	AWS Trusted Acvisor

Explanation

An online resource to benefit you reduce cost, rise performance, and improve security by optimizing your Amazon web services environment, Trusted Advisor provides real-time guidance to help you provision your resources following Amazon web services best practices.

417.

a)	VPC Flow Logs

Explanation

VPC Flow Logs is a feature that allows you to capture data about the IP traffic going to and from network interfaces in VPC. Flow log data is kept using Amazon CloudWatch Logs. After you have created a flow log, you can view and retrieve its data in Amazon CloudWatch Logs.

418.

    a)   Enable cross region snapshots for the redshift cluster

Explanation

You can configure cross-regional snapshot when you want Amazon Redshift to automatically copy snapshot to another region for backup purpose. Note that copying snapshots from the source region to a destination region incurs data transfer charges.

419.

    a)   Enable read replicas for the database

Explanation

Amazon Read Replicas allow you to make one or more read-only copies of your DB instance within the same Amazon web services Region or in a different Amazon web services Region. Updates made to the source DB are then asynchronously copied to your Read Replicas. In addition to giving scalability for read-heavy workloads, Read Replicas can be promoted to become a standalone DB instance when required.

420.

    a) Post your log data to an Amazon Kinesis data stream, and subscribe your log-processing application, so that is configured to process your logging data.

Explanation

Amazon Kinesis makes it easy to process, collect, and analyze real-time, streaming data so you can get timely insights and react quickly to innovative information. Amazon Kinesis offers key capabilities to cost-effective process streaming data at any scale, along with the flexibility to select the tools that best suit the desires of your application. With Amazon Kinesis, you can ingest real-time data like application logs, website clickstreams, and more into your databases, data lakes, IoT telemetry data and data warehouses, or build your own real-time applications by this data. Amazon Kinesis enables you to process and analyze data as it arrives and responds in real time instead of having to wait until all your data is collected before the processing can begin.

421.

    a) Create an Amazon machine image

Explanation

An Amazon Machine Image gives the information required to launch an instance, which is a virtual server in the cloud. You have to specify a source Amazon Machine Image when you start an instance. You can launch many instances from a single Amazon Machine Image when you want multiple instances with the same configuration. You can use different Amazon Machine Images to launch instances when you want instances with different configurations.

422.
   a) Direct Connect
   b) Snowball

Explanation

With a Snowball, you can transfer hundreds of petabytes or terabytes of data between your on-premises data centers and Amazon Simple Storage Service. Amazon web services Snowball use Snowball appliances and gives powerful interfaces that you can utilize to transfer data, create jobs, and track the status of your jobs through to completion. By transferring your data in Snowballs, you can transfer big amounts of data at a significantly faster time than if you were transferring that information over the Internet, saving you time as well as cash.

Amazon web services Direct Connect links your internal network to an Amazon web services Direct Connect location over a standard 1 gigabit to 10 gigabit Ethernet fiber optic cable. One end of cable is connected to router, the other to an Amazon web services Direct Connect router. With this connection in place, you can make directly to public Amazon web services or to Amazon VPC, avoiding Internet service providers in your network route.

423.
   a)   Modify the VPC security group

Explanation

Any cluster that you makes is closed to everyone. Identity and access management credentials only control access to the Amazon Redshift API related resources. The Amazon Redshift console, command line interface, SDK, and API. To allow access to the cluster from SQL user tools via JDBC or ODBC.

You use security groups:

   • If you are using the EC2 Classic platform for your Amazon Redshift cluster, you must use Amazon Redshift security groups.
   • If you are using the EC2 VPC platform for your Amazon Redshift cluster, you must use VPC security groups.

424.
   a)   Amazon kinesis

Explanation

Amazon Kinesis makes it easy to process, collect, and analyze real-time, streaming data so you could get timely insights and react rapidly to new information. Amazon Kinesis offers keys capabilities to cost-effectively process streaming information at any scale, along with the flexibility to select the tools that suit the needs of your application. With Amazon Kinesis, you can ingest real-time data such as audio, video, application logs, website clickstreams, and IoT telemetry data for machine learning, analytics, and other applications. Amazon Kinesis enables you to process and analyze data as it arrives and responds instantly instead of having to wait till all your data is collected before the processing can begin.

425.
   a)   Security groups

Explanation

A security group acts as a virtual firewall for your instance to control outbound and inbound traffic. When you start an instance in a VPC, you can assign up to 5 security groups to the instance. Security groups act on the instance level, not the subnet level. Therefore, every instance in a subnet in your VPC could be assigned to a dissimilar set of security groups. If you do not specify a particular group at start time, the instance is automatically allocated to the by default security group for the VPC.

426.
   a)   AWS ESB volumes

Explanation

For block-level storage, consider EBS volume

Options B & C are incorrect since they are providing object level storage

Option D is incorrect since this provides file-level storage

427.
   a)   EBS cold HDD

Explanation

EBS cold HDD

Low-cost HDD volume designed for less frequently accessed workloads

- Throughput-oriented storage for a large volume of data that is infrequently accessed
- Scenarios where the low storage cost is important

- Can not be a boot volume

428.

    a) AWS CloudWatch Logs

Explanation

You can use Amazon CloudWatch Logs to monitor, store, and access your log files from Amazon Elastic Compute Cloud (Amazon EC2) instances, AWS CloudTrail, and other sources.

429.

    a) Reserved instances

Explanation

When you have instances that will be used continuously, and throughout the year, the best option is to buy reserved instances. By buying reserved instances, you are actually allocated an instance for the entire year or the duration you specify with a reduced cost.

430.

    a) Amazon S3 is highly available and fault tolerant by design and requires no additional configuration

Explanation

AWS S3 is already highly available and fault tolerant by design and requires no additional configuration

431.

    a) Amazon Glacier

Explanation

Amazon Glacier is a secure, durable, and extremely low-cost cloud storage service for data archiving and long-term backup. It is designed to deliver 99.99999% durability and gives comprehensive security and compliance capabilities that can help meet even the most stringent regulator needs.

432.

    a) Single Amazon S3 bucket

Explanation

Amazon S3 is the best storage option for this. It is durable and highly available

433.
   a)   The auto-scaling groups scale up policy has not yet been reached
   b)   You already have 20 on demand instances running

Explanation

You can run up to 20 On-Demand EC2 instances. If you need more, you have to complete a requisition form and submit it to AWS.

However, in the question, we have already mentioned that MAX is set to 10. In that case, option B is invalid and hence cannot be marked as an answer. But the question does not mention that the metric chosen for this Auto Scaling policy is CPUUtilization Metric. It could be DiskWrites or Network In/Out metric. Assuming the current set up is to do with a metric other than CPUUtilization we can choose option D as a right choice. In this scenario, we are only discussing about the non-functioning Scaling up the process and not about the Scaling down scenario.

434.
   a)   Increasing the cache expiration time

Explanation

You can control how long objects stay in a CloudFront cache before CloudFront forwards another request to your origin. Decreasing the period allows you to serve dynamic content. Increasing the period means your client get better performance because your objects are more likely to be served straight from the edge cache. A longer period also reduces the load on your origin.

435.
   a) Backup and restore

Explanation

Since the cost needs to be at a minimum, the best option is to back up all the resources and then perform a restore in the event of a disaster.

436.
   a) Migrate the NAT instance to NAT gateway and host the NAT gateway in the public subnet

Explanation

One can simply start using the NAT Gateway service and stop using the deployed NAT instances. But you need to ensure that the NAT Gateway is deployed in the public subnet.

437.
   a) Enable the logs on the ELB and then investigate the logs whenever there is an issue

b) Use cloudwatch for monitoring

Explanation

Elastic Load Balancing gives access logs that capture detailed information about requests directed to your load balancer. Each log have information such as the time of the request was received, the clients IP address, latencies, request paths, and server responses. You can utilize these access logs to analyze traffic patterns and to troubleshoot the issue.

438.

a) Configure storage gateway stored volume

Explanation

If you require low latency access to your entire dataset, first configure your on-premises gateway to store all your data locally. Then asynchronously back up a point in time snapshots of this data to Amazon S3. This configuration gives durable and inexpensive offsite backups that you can recover to your local data center or Amazon EC2.

439.

a)   VPC Endpoint

Explanation

A VPC endpoint allows you to privately connect your VPC to supported Amazon web services and VPC endpoint services powered by PrivateLink without needing an internet gateway, NAT device, VPN connection, or Amazon web services Direct Connect connection. Instances in your VPC don't need public IP addresses to communicate with resources in the service. Traffic between your VPC and the other service doesn't leave the Amazon network.

440.

a)   Use a public subnet for the web tier and a private subnet for the database layer

Explanation

The ideal setup is to ensure that the web server is hosted on the public subnet so that it can be accessed by users on the internet. The database server can be hosted in the private subnet.

441.

a)   Use server-side Encryption for S3
b)   Use SSL/HTTPS when using the elastic load balancer
c)   Encrypt all EBS volume attached to EC2 Instances

Explanation

Amazon EBS encryption offers you a simple encryption solution for your EBS volumes without the need for you to build, maintain, and secure your personal key management infrastructure. When you make an encrypted EBS volume and attach it to a supported instance type.

The following types of data are encrypted:

- All snapshots created from the volume
- All Information is moving between the volume and the instance
- Data at rest inside the volume

Data protection refers to protecting data while in-transit and at rest. You can protect data in transit by utilizing SSL or by utilizing client-side encryption. You have the following options for protecting data at rest in Amazon S3.

- Use Server-Side Encryption – You request Amazon S3 to encrypt your object before saving it on disks in its data centers and decode it when you download the objects.
- Use Client-Side Encryption – You can encrypt data client-side and upload the encode data to Amazon S3. In such case, you manage the encryption process, the encryption keys, and related tools.

You can create a load balancer that customs the SSL/TLS protocol for the encrypted connection. This feature allows traffic encryption between your load balancer and the user that initiate (HTTPS) sessions, and for links between your load balancer and your EC2 instances.

442.
   a)   Use CloudWatch metrics to check the utilization of the web layer. Use Auto Scaling Group to scale the web instances accordingly based on the CloudWatch metrics.
   b)   Utilize the Multi AZ feature for the Amazon RDS layer

Explanation

Amazon RDS Multi AZ deployments give enhanced availability and durability for Database Instances, making them a natural fit for production DB workloads. When you provision a Multi AZ database Instance, Amazon RDS automatically makes a primary database Instance and synchronously duplicates the data to a standby instance in a dissimilar Availability Zone. Each Availability Zone runs on its personal physically distinct, independent infrastructure, and is engineered to be extremely reliable. In case of infrastructure failure, Amazon relational database performs an automatic failover to the standby, so that you can continue database operations as soon as the failover is complete. Since the endpoint for your database Instance remains same after a failover, your

application can continue DB operation without the requirement for manual administrative intervention.

443.
a) Use an S3 bucket policy that ensures that MFA Delete is set on the objects in the bucket.

b) Create an IAM Role and ensure the EC2 Instances use the IAM Role to access the data in the bucket.

Explanation

IAM roles are designed so that your applications can securely make API requests from your instances, without needing you to manage the security credentials that the applications use. Instead of creating and distributing your Amazon web services credentials, you can delegate permission to make API requests using IAM Roles

444.
a) AWS Config

Explanation

With Amazon web services Config, you can do the following:

• Evaluate your Amazon web services resource configurations for desired settings.
• Get a snapshot of the existing configurations of the supported resources that are associated with your Amazon web services account.
• Retrieve configurations of one or many resources that exist in your account.
• Receive a notification every time a resource is created, deleted, or modified.
• View relationships between resources.
• Retrieve historical configuration of one or more resources

445.
a) Create Amazon DB Read Replicas. Configure the application layer to query the Read Replicas for query needs.

b) Use elasticache in front of your Amazon RDS DB to cache common queries

Explanation

Amazon RDS Read Replicas gives enhanced performance and durability for database instances. This replication feature makes it easy to elastically scale out beyond the capacity constraints of a single DB Instance for read-heavy database workloads. You can create one or more replicas of a given source DB Instance and serve high-volume application read traffic from multiple copies of your data, thereby increasing aggregate read throughput. Read replicas can also be promoted when needed to become standalone DB instances.

Amazon ElastiCache is a web service that makes it easy to deploy, operate, and scale an in-memory data store or cache in the cloud. The service improves the performance of web applications by allowing you to retrieve information from fast, managed, in-memory data stores, instead of relying entirely on slower disk-based databases.

446.

    a) Ensure that the security groups have the required rules defined to allow traffic

Explanation

Option A is invalid since the route tables would already have the required rules to route traffic between subnets in a VPC

447.

    a) Create a role which has the necessary and can be assumed by the EC2 instance.

Explanation

Identity and access management roles are designed in such a way so that your applications can securely make API requests from your instances, without requiring you to manage the security credentials that the applications use.

448.

    a) Use the multi AZ feature for the database
    b) Ensure that automated backups are enabled for the RDS

Explanation

Amazon RDS Multi AZ deployments give enhanced availability and durability for Database Instances, making them a natural fit for production DB workloads. When you provision a Multi AZ database Instance, Amazon RDS automatically makes a primary database Instance and synchronously replicates the information to a standby instance in a different Availability Zone. Each Availability Zone runs on its personal physically distinct, independent infrastructure, and is engineered to be highly reliable. In case of infrastructure failure, Amazon relational database performs an automatic failover to the standby, so that you can resume database operations as soon as the failover is complete.

Amazon RDS creates and saves automated backups of your DB instance. Amazon RDS creates a storage volume snapshot of your DB instance, backing up the entire DB instance and not just individual databases.

449.

    a) AWS ECS

Explanation

Amazon Elastic Container Service is a highly scalable, high-performance container orchestration service that supports Docker containers and enables you to easily run and scale containerized applications on Amazon web services. Amazon ECS eliminates the want for you to install and operate your personal container orchestration software, control and scale a cluster of virtual machines, or schedule containers on those virtual machines.

450.
    a) Create a base AMI

Explanation

An Amazon Machine Image gives the information needed to launch an instance, which is a virtual server in the cloud. You have to specify a source AMI when you start an instance. You can start multiple instances from a single AMI when you want multiple instances with the similar configuration. You can use dissimilar AMIs to launch instances when you want instances with unique configurations.

451.
    a) Amazon elastic load balancing
    b) Amazon elastic compute cloud (EC2)

Explanation

Elastic Load Balancing automatically issues incoming application traffic across multiple targets, like Amazon EC2 instances, containers, and IP addresses. It can handle the varying load of your application traffic in a single AZ (Availability Zone) or across multiple AZ. Elastic Load Balancing offers 3 types of load balancers that all feature the high availability, automatic scaling, and robust security necessary to make your applications fault tolerant.

The ELB and EC2 instances get setup for high availability. You have the ELB placed in front of the instances.

For more information

https://aws.amazon.com/elasticloadbalancing/

452.
    a) AWS SQS for distributed processing of messages by the worker process
    b) AWS simple storage service for storing the videos and images

Explanation

Amazon Simple Storage Service is storage for the Internet. It is designed to make web-scale computing easier for developers.

Amazon Simple Queue Service (SQS) is a fully managed message queuing service that enables you to decouple and scale microservices, distributed systems, and serverless applications. SQS eliminates the complexity and overhead associated with managing and

operating message-oriented middleware and empowers developers to focus on differentiating work. Using SQS, you can send, store, and receive messages between software components at any volume, without losing messages or requiring other services to be available.

453.
   a) All instances launched with a public IP
   b) Route table entry added for the internet gateway
   c) An internet gateway attached to the VPC

Explanation

VPC with a Single Public Subnet:

The configuration for this scenario contains a virtual private cloud with a single public subnet, and an Internet gateway to allow communication over the Internet. We recommend this configuration if you want to run a single-tier, public-facing web application, such as a blog or a simple website.

For more Information, please visit

https://docs.aws.amazon.com/vpc/latest/userguide/VPC_Scenario1.html

454.
   a) A private subnet for the database tier
   b) A public subnet for the database tier

Explanation

VPC with Public and Private Subnets (NAT):

The configuration for this scenario contains a virtual private cloud with a private subnet and a public subnet. We recommend this situation if you need to run a public-facing web application, while maintaining back-end servers that are not publicly accessible. A common example is a multi-tier website, with the web servers in a public subnet and the database servers in a private subnet. You can set up security and routing so that the web servers can communicate with the database servers.

For more information on private and public subnets and the VPC, please visit the below URL:

https://docs.aws.amazon.com/vpc/latest/userguide/VPC_Scenario2.html

455.

a) Creating snapshot of the EBS volumes
b) Ensure the snapshots are made available in another region

Explanation

You can back up the data on Amazon EBS volumes to Amazon S3 by taking a point in time snapshots. Snapshots are incremental backups, that means that only the blocks on the device that have changed after your most newest snapshot are saved. This minimizes the period required to make the snapshot and saves on storage money by not duplicating data. When you remove a snapshot, only the data unique to that snapshot is deleted. Each snapshot has all of the information required to restore your data to a new EBS volume.

456.
a) Multiple availability zones
b) Elastic load balancer
c) An auto scaling group to recover from EC2 instance failures

Explanation

1) ELB which is placed in front of the users which helps in directing the traffic to the EC2 Instances.
2) The EC2 Instances which are placed as part of an AutoScaling Group
3) And then you have multiple subnets which are mapped to multiple availability zones

For a static web site, the SQS is not required to build such an environment. If you have a system such as an order processing system, which has that sort of queuing of requests, then that could be a candidate for using SQS Queues.

457.
a)   Enable cross-region replication for the underlying bucket

Explanation

Cross region replication is a bucket level configuration that allows automatic, asynchronous copying of objects across buckets in different Amazon web services Regions. We refer to these buckets. These buckets can be owned by different Amazon web services accounts.

458.
a)   Create a snapshot of the volume and then create a volume from the snapshot in the other AZ

Explanation

Option A is invalid because the Instance and Volume have to be in the same AZ for it to be attached to the instance.

459.
  a)   Create 2 private subnet for the backend instances
  b)   Create 2 public subnet for the Elastic load balancer

Explanation

You must create public subnets in the same Availability Zones as the private subnets that are used by your private instances. Then associate these public subnets to the Internet-facing load balancer.

460.
  a)   AWS Trusted Advisor

Explanation

An online resource to help you minimize cost, increase performance, and improve security by optimizing your Amazon web services environment, Trusted Advisor gives real-time guidance to benefit you provision your resources following Amazon web services best practices.

461.
  a) AWS Cloudformation

Explanation

Amazon web services CloudFormation is a service that benefits you model and set up your AWS resources so that you can spend fewer time managing those resources and extra time focusing on your applications that run in Amazon web services. You make a template that describes all the Amazon web services resources that you want, and Amazon web services CloudFormation takes care of provisioning and configuring those resources for you.

462.
  a) Create a bastion host in the public subnet. Make IT admin staff use this as a jump server to the backend instances.

Explanation

A bastion host is a server whose responsibility is to give access to a private network from an external network, like the Internet. Because of its experience to potential attack, a bastion host must minimize the chances of penetration.

463.
  a) Allow Inbound access on port 433 for 0.0.0.0/0

Explanation

A security group acts as a virtual firewall for instance to control inbound and outbound traffic. When you start an instance in a VPC, you can assign up to 5 security groups to the

instance. Security groups act at the instance level, not the subnet level. Therefore, each instance in a subnet in VPC could be assigned to a different set of security groups. If you do not identify a particular group at start time, the instance is automatically assigned to the by default security group for the VPC.

464.

a) Using a Curl or Get Command to get the latest meta-data from http://169.254.169.254/latest/meta-data/

Explanation

To get the private and public IP addresses, you can run the following commands on the running instance

- http://169.254.169.254/latest/meta-data/local-ipv4
- http://169.254.169.254/latest/meta-data/public-ipv4

465.

a) Outputs

Explanation

The below example shows a simple CloudFormation template. It creates an EC2 instance based on the AMI - ami-d6f32ab5. When the instance is created, it will output the AZ in which it is created.

```
{
  "Resources": {
    "MyEC2Instance": {
      "Type": "AWS::EC2::Instance",
      "Properties": {
        "ImageId": "ami-d6f32ab5"
      }
    }
  },
  "Outputs": {
    "Availability": {
      "Description": "The Instance ID",
      "Value":
      { "Fn::GetAtt" : [ "MyEC2Instance", "AvailabilityZone" ]}
    }
  }
}
```

466.

a) VPN connection

Explanation

By default, instances that you launch into an Amazon VPC can't communicate with your own (remote) network. You can enable access to your remote network from your VPC by attaching a virtual private gateway to the VPC, making a custom route table, updating your security group rules, and creating an AWS managed VPN connection.

467.
   a) Provisioned IOPS

Explanation

Provisioned IOPS:

Highest performance SSD volume designed for latency sensitive transactional workloads

For information on the different EBS volume types, please visit the below URL

https://aws.amazon.com/ebs/details/

468.
   a) Create cloudwatch alarm that stops and start the instance based off of status check alarm

Explanation

Using Amazon CloudWatch alarm actions, you can create alarms that automatically stop, terminate, reboot, or recover your EC2 instances. You can utilize the stop or dismiss actions to help you save cash when you no longer required an instance to be running. You can utilize the restart and recover actions to automatically restart those instances or recover them onto new hardware if a system impairment occurs.

469.
   a) AWS DynamoDB
   b) AWS S3

Explanation

Amazon DynamoDB is a fully managed NoSQL DB service that gives a fast and predictable performance with smooth scalability. DynamoDB allows you to offload the administrative burdens of operating and scaling a distributed DB so that you do not have to concern about hardware provisioning, setup, and configuration, cluster scaling, replication, software patching.

470.
   a) Enable S3 Server-side Encryption
   b) Enable EBS Encryption

Explanation

Amazon elastic block storage encryption offers a simple encryption solution for your elastic block storage volumes without the requirement to build, maintain, and secure your personal key management infrastructure.

Server-side encryption protects data at rest. Server-side encryption with Amazon S3 managed encryption keys SSE-S3 uses strong multi-factor encryption.

471.
a) Use the WAF service in front of the web application

Explanation

Amazon web services WAF is a web application firewall that helps guard your web applications from common web exploits that could affect application availability, compromise security, or consume excessive resources. Amazon web services WAF provides you control over which traffic to enable or block to your web applications by defining customizable web security rules. You can utilize Amazon web services WAF to create clients rules that block common attack patterns, like SQL injection or cross-site scripting, and rules that are designed for your specific application.

472.
a) An SQS queue as the messaging component between the instances and servers

Explanation

Amazon SQS is a fully managed message queuing service that allows you to decouple and scale microservices, serverless applications, and distributed systems. Amazon SQS eliminates the complexity and overhead associated with managing and operating message-oriented middleware and empowers developers to focus on differentiating work. Using Amazon SQS, you can send, receive, and store messages between software components at any volume, without losing messages or needing other services to be available.

473.
a) User service control policies
b) Use AWS organization

Explanation

With Amazon web services Organizations, you can centrally manage policies across multiple Amazon web services accounts without having to usage custom scripts and manual processes. For instance, you can apply service control policies across multiple Amazon web services accounts that are members of an organization. Service control policies enable you to define which Amazon web services APIs can and cannot be executed

by Amazon web services Identity and Access Management entities in your organization's member Amazon web services accounts. Service control policies are created and applied to the master account, which is the Amazon web services account that you utilized when you created your organization.

474.
a) Ensuring that no on-premises communication is required via transitive routing
b) Ensuring that the VPC's do not have overlapping CIDR blocks

Explanation

You have a VPC peering connection between VPC A and VPC B (pcx-aaaabbbb). VPC A also has a VPN connection or an Amazon web services Direct Connect connection to a corporate network. Edge to edge routing is not supported. You can't use VPC A to extend the peering relationship to exist between VPC B and the corporate network.

For information on Invalid peering configurations, please refer to the below link

https://docs.aws.amazon.com/vpc/latest/peering/invalid-peering-configurations.html

475.
a) A virtual private gateway attached to the VPC
b) A public IP address on the customer gateway for the on-premises network

Explanation

AWS Managed VPN Connections:

By default, instances that you starts into an Amazon VPC can not communicate with your own network. You can allow access to your remote network from your VPC by attaching a virtual private gateway to the VPC, making a custom route table, updating your security group rules, and creating an Amazon web services managed VPN connection.

This is mentioned in the Amazon web services documentation. For more information on VPN connections, please refer to the below link

https://docs.aws.amazon.com/vpc/latest/userguide/VPC_VPN.html

476.
a) Use the HSM module

Explanation

Amazon web services CloudHSM is a cloud-based hardware security module HSM that allows you to easily generate and use your personal encryption keys on the Amazon web services Cloud. With CloudHSM, you can manage your personal encryption keys using FIPS 140-2 Level three validated HSMs

477.
   a) AWS DynamoDB

Explanation

Amazon DynamoDB is an entirely managed NoSQL database service that offers fast and predictable performance with smooth scalability. DynamoDB allows you to offload the administrative burdens of operating and scaling a distributed DB so that you don't have to worry about configuration, hardware provisioning, setup, software patching, replication, or cluster scaling. It is ideal for storing JSON based objects

478.
   a) Ensure to modify the security group
   b) Ensure that the instance has a public or elastic IP

Explanation

To enable access to or from the internet for instances in a VPC subnet, you must do the following:

- Ensure that your network access control and security group rules allow the relevant traffic to flow to and from your instance.
- Ensure that instances in your subnet have a worldwide unique IP address.
- Ensure that subnet's route table points to the internet gateway.
- Attach an internet gateway to your VPC

479.
   a) Maintain a single snapshot the latest snapshot is both incremental and complete

Explanation

You can back up the information on your Amazon elastic block storage volumes to Amazon S3 by taking a point in time snapshots. Snapshots are incremental backups, which means that the blocks on the device that have changed after your recent snapshot are saved. This minimizes the period required to make the snapshot and saves on storage costs by not duplicating data. When you remove a snapshot, the data unique to that snapshot is eliminated. Each snapshot has all of the information required to restore your data to a new elastic block storage volume.

480.
   a) Consider using provisioned IOPS Volumes
   b) Use a large EC2 instance

Explanation

IOPS Volume:

Highest performance SSD volume designed for latency sensitive transactional workloads.

The AWS Documentation shows different volume types and why Provisioned IOPS is the most ideal for this requirement. For more information on the different EBS volume types, please visit the below URL

https://aws.amazon.com/ebs/details/

481.

    a) You are disabling the point in time recovery

Explanation

Amazon RDS makes a storage volume snapshot of your database instance, backing up the entire database instance and not just individual databases. You can set the backup retention duration when you make a DB instance. If you do not set the backup retention time, Amazon RDS utilize a default period retention duration of 1 day. You can modify the backup retention duration valid values are to a maximum of 35 days

482.

    a) Place a CloudFront distribution in front of the web application

Explanation

Amazon CloudFront is a worldwide content delivery network service that securely delivers data, applications, videos, and APIs to your viewers with short latency and great transfer speeds. CloudFront is integrated with Amazon web services including physical locations that are directly connected to the Amazon web services global infrastructure, as well as software that works seamlessly with services including Amazon web services Shield for (DDoS) mitigation, Amazon S3, Elastic Load Balancing or Amazon EC2 as origins for your apps, and Lambda@Edge to run custom code close to your viewers.

483.

    a) Create an alias for CNAME record to the load balancer DNS name
    b) Ensure that a hosted zone is in place

Explanation

While ordinary Amazon Route 53 records are standard DNS records, alias records give a Route 53–specific extension to Domain name system functionality. Instead of an IP address or a (DN), an alias record contains a pointer to an Amazon web services resource such as a CloudFront distribution or an Amazon S3 bucket. When Route 53 receives a domain name system query that matches the name and type in a record, Route 53 keep an eye on the pointer and responds with the applicable value:

- Amazon S3 bucket that is designed as a static website Route 53 responds to each query with one IP address for the AWS S3 bucket.
- An ELB load balancerRoute53 responds to each query with one or more IP addresses for the load balancer.
- An Elastic Beanstalk environment_Route 53 responds to each query with one or more IP addresses for the environment.
- An alternate domain name (DN) for a CloudFront distribution Route 53 responds as if the query had asked for the CloudFront distribution by the CloudFront domain name, such as d11111abcdef8.cloudfront.net.

484.
  a) Deploy elasticache in front of the database server

Explanation

Amazon elasticache deals fully managed Redis and Memcached. Seamlessly deploy, scale, and operate popular open source compatible in-memory data stores. Build data-intensive applications or improve the performance of your existing applications by retrieving data from high throughput and low latency in-memory data stores.

485.
  a) Enable multi AZ failover

Explanation

Amazon RDS Multi AZ deployments give enhanced availability and durability for Database Instances, making them a natural fit for production database workloads. When you provision a Multi AZ database Instance, Amazon RDS automatically makes a primary database Instance and synchronously replicates the information to a standby instance in a dissimilar Availability Zone. Each Availability Zone (AZ) runs on its own independent infrastructure, physically distinct, and is engineered to be highly reliable. In the situation of infrastructure failure, Amazon (RDS) performs an automatic failover to the standby, so that you can continue database operations as soon as the failover is done.

486.
  a) AWS cloudwatch

Explanation

Amazon CloudWatch is a management and monitoring service built for developers, site reliability engineers, system operators, and IT managers. CloudWatch gives you with data and actionable insights to monitor your applications, understand and respond to system-wide performance changes, optimize resource utilization, and get a unified view of operational health. CloudWatch gathers monitoring and operational data in the form of

metrics, logs, and events, providing you with a unified view of Amazon web services resources, applications, and services that run on Amazon web services, and on-premises servers.

487.
   a) Store the data on S3 and then use Lifecycle policies to transfer the data to Amazon Glacier

Explanation

To manage your objects so that they are kept cost-effectively throughout their lifecycle, configure their lifecycle. A lifecycle configuration is a set of rule that describes actions that Amazon S3 applies to a group of objects.

There are two types of actions:

   • Expiration actions_define when objects expire. Amazon S3 removes expired objects on your behalf.

   • Transition actions_Define when objects transition to another storage class. For instance, you might choose to transition objects to the STANDARD IA storage class one month after you made them, or archive objects to the GLACIER storage class 1 year after creating them.

488.
   a) SQS should be used to facilitate horizontal scaling of encoding tasks

Explanation

Amazon SQS offers a secure, durable, and available hosted queue that lets you integrate and decouple distributed software systems and components.

489.
   a) Adjust the instance's security group to permit ingress traffic over port 22 from your IP

Explanation

Security groups turn as a virtual firewall that controls the traffic for one or many instances. When you start an instance, you associate one or many security groups with the instance. You add rules to a security group that let traffic to or from its associated instances.

490.
   a) Remove public read access and use signed URLs with expiry dates

Explanation

A pre signed URL provides you access to the object identified in the URL, providing that the creator of the pre signed URL has permissions to access that object. That is if you

receive a pre signed URL to upload an object. You could upload the object only if the creator of the pre signed URL has the necessary permissions to upload that object.

491.

   a) AWS OpsWorks

Explanation

Amazon web services OpsWorks is a configuration management service that provides managed instances of Chef and Puppet. Chef and Puppet are automation platforms that allow you to use code to automate the configurations of your servers. OpsWorks lets you use Chef and Puppet to automate how servers are configured, deployed and managed across your Amazon EC2 instances or on-premises compute environments. OpsWorks has three offerings, AWS Opsworks for Chef Automate, AWS OpsWorks for Puppet Enterprise, and AWS OpsWorks Stacks.

492.

   a) AWS cloudformation

Explanation

Amazon web services CloudFormation is a service that benefits you model and set up your AWS resources so that you can spend less interval managing those resources and more time focusing on your applications that run in Amazon web services. You make a template that describes all the Amazon web services resources that you want and Amazon web services CloudFormation takes care of provisioning and configuring those resources for any one. You don't need to individually create and configure Amazon web services resources and figure out what's dependent on what Amazon web services CloudFormation handles all of that.

493.

   e) Cluster placement group

Explanation

Cluster placement groups are suggested for applications that benefit from high network throughput, low network latency, or both and if the majority of the network traffic is between the instances in the groups. To gives the lowest latency and the highest packet-per-second network performance for your placement group, choose an instance type that supports enhanced networking

494.

   a) Add an event notification to the S3 bucket
   b) Create an SNS topic

Explanation

The Amazon S3 notification feature enables you to receive notifications when certain events happen in your bucket. To enable notifications, you must first add a notification configuration identifying the events you want Amazon S3 to publish, and the destinations where you want Amazon S3 to send the event notifications.

495.

a)   AWS Lambda

Explanation

Amazon web services Lambda is a compute service that lets you run code without provisioning or managing servers. Amazon web services Lambda executes your code only when needed and scales automatically, from a few requests per day to thousands per second. You pay only for the compute period you consume - there is no charge when your code is not running. With Amazon web services Lambda, you can run code for virtually any type of application or backend service - all with zero administration

496.

a)   Create a separate VPC peering connection from Development to Production and from Test to the Production VPC

Explanation

A VPC peering connection is a networking connection between 2 VPCs that allows you to route traffic between them utilizing private IPv6 addresses or IPv4 addresses. Instances in either VPC can communicate with each other as if they are within the similar network. You can make a VPC peering connection between your personal VPCs, or with a VPC in another Amazon web services account.

You can peer the VPC's as mentioned in the AWS documentation. For more information on VPC peering, please visit the URL

https://docs.aws.amazon.com/vpc/latest/peering/what-is-vpc-peering.html

497.

a)   Determining the minimum memory requirements for an application

Explanation

You should decide on what are requirements for the underlying EC2 Instance. You can then choose the Instance type for the underlying EC2 Instance

498.

a) DynamoDB

Explanation

Amazon DynamoDB is a nonrelational database that delivers reliable performance at any scale. It's a fully managed, multi-region, multi-master database that provides consistent single-digit millisecond latency, and offers built-in security, backup and restore, and in-memory caching.

499.
   a) Ensure that server-side encryption is enabled for an S3 bucket
   b) Ensure that all EBS volume is encrypted

Explanation

Amazon elastic block storage encryption offers a simple encryption solution for your EBS volumes without the need to build, maintain, and secure your own key management infrastructure.

Server-side encryption protects data at rest. Server-side encryption with Amazon S3 managed encryption keys SSE-S3 uses strong multi-factor encryption. Amazon S3 encrypts separate object with a unique key

500.
   a) Use a load balancer in front of the EC2 instances
   b) Ensure that the EC2 instances are spread across multiple availability zones

Explanation

Elastic Load Balancing distributes incoming application or network traffic across multiple targets, like Amazon EC2 instances, containers, and IP addresses, in multiple AZ. Elastic Load Balancing scales your load balancer as traffic to your application changes over time, and can scale to the huge majority of workloads automatically.

This is clearly mentioned in the AWS Documentation, for more information, please visit following URL

https://docs.aws.amazon.com/elasticloadbalancing/latest/userguide/what-is-load-balancing.html

501.
   a) AWS VPN

Explanation

AWS Managed VPN:

You can make an IPsec VPN connection between your VPC and your remote network. On the Amazon web services side of the VPN connection, a virtual private gateway gives two

VPN endpoints for automatic failover. You configure your customer gateway on the remote side of the VPN connection.

AWS VPN CloudHub:

If you have many remote network (for example, multiple branch offices), you can make multiple Amazon web services managed VPN connections via your virtual private gateway to allow communication between these networks.

IPSec is used for encryption of traffic in the VPN connection, for more information kindly use this URL

https://docs.aws.amazon.com/vpc/latest/userguide/vpn-connections.html

502.
  a) Create an AMI and copy it to another region

Explanation

AMI (Amazon Machine Images) are preconfigured with operating systems, and some preconfigured Amazon Machine Images might also include application stacks. You can also configure your own Amazon Machine Images. In the context of DR, we intensely recommend that you identify and configure your own Amazon Machine Images so that they can launch as part of your recovery procedure. Such Amazon Machine Images should be preconfigured with your operating system of choice plus appropriate pieces of the application stack.

503.
  a) Enable CRR for the bucket

Explanation

Cross region replication is a bucket level configuration that enables automatic, asynchronous copying of objects across buckets in different Amazon web services Regions. We mention to these buckets as source bucket and destination bucket. These buckets can be owned by different Amazon web services accounts.

504.
  a) Reserved instances

Explanation

Amazon EC2 gives the following purchasing options to allow you to optimize your costs based on your needs:

  • Dedicated Instances Pay by the hour, for instances that run on single-tenant hardware.

- Dedicated Hosts Pay for a physical host that is fully dedicated to running your instances, and bring you're existing per socket, per core, or per VM software licenses to reduce costs.
- Spot Instances Request unused (EC2) instances, which can lesser your Amazon (EC2) costs significantly.
- Scheduled Instances-Purchase instances that are always available on the specified recurring schedule, for a one-year term.
- Reserved Instances Purchase at an important discount, instances that are always available, for a term from 1 to 3 years.

505.
  a) Create a cloudwatch matric which looks at the desired metric and then restarts the server based on the threshold

Explanation

Utilizing Amazon CloudWatch alarm actions, you can make alarms that automatically reboot, terminate, stop, or recover your EC2 instances. You can utilize the stop or terminate actions to help you save money when you no longer required an instance to be running. You can utilize the recover and reboot actions to automatically restart those instances or recover them onto hardware if a system impairment occurs.

506.
  a) Enable read replica's and offload the reads to the replica's

Explanation

Amazon RDS Read Replicas gives enhanced performance and durability for database instances. This replication feature makes it easy to elastically scale out beyond the capacity constraints of a single database Instance for read-heavy database workloads. You can make one or more replicas of a given source DB Instance and serve high volume application read traffic from many copies of your data, thereby increasing aggregate read throughput. Read replicas can also be promoted when required to become standalone DB instances.

507.
  a) AWS DynamoDB

Explanation

Amazon DynamoDB is a non-relational database that delivers reliable performance at any scale. It's a fully managed, multi-region, multi-master database that provides consistent single-digit millisecond latency, and offers built-in security, backup and restore, and in-memory caching.

508.

a) Amazon SNS
b) Amazon CloudWatch

Explanation

You can monitor DB instances using Amazon CloudWatch, which collects and processes raw data from Amazon RDS into readable, close real-time metrics. These statistics are verified for a period of 2 weeks so that you can access historical data and gain a better perspective on how your web app or service is performing.

509.

a) Use lifecycle policies to transfer the files onto glacier after a period of 2 months

Explanation

To manage your objects so that they are stored cost-effectively throughout their lifecycle, configure their lifecycle. A lifecycle configuration is a set of rulebooks that define actions that Amazon S3 applies to a group of objects. There are two types of actions:

- Expiration actions Define when objects expire. Amazon S3 deletes expired objects on your behalf. The lifecycle expiration costs depend on when you choose to expire objects.

- Transition actions Define when objects transition to another storage class.

510.

a) NAT Gateway

Explanation

You can use a network address translation (NAT) gateway to enable instances in a private subnet to attach to the internet or other Amazon web service but prevent the internet from initiating a connection with those instances

About Our Products

Other products from IPSpecialist LTD regarding AWS technology are:

 AWS Certified Cloud Practitioner Technology Workbook

 AWS Certified Solution Architect - Associate Workbook

Upcoming products from IPSpecialist LTD regarding AWS technology are:

 AWS Certified DevOps Associate Technology Workbook

 AWS Certified DevOps Engineer - Professional Technology Workbook

 AWS Certified Solution Architect - Professional Technology Workbook

 AWS Certified Advance Networking – Specialty Technology Workbook

 AWS Certified Big Data – Specialty Technology Workbook

Note from the Author:

Reviews are gold to authors! If you have enjoyed this book and it helped you along certification, would you consider rating it and reviewing it?

Link to Product Page:

www.ingramcontent.com/pod-product-compliance
Lightning Source LLC
Chambersburg PA
CBHW060533060326
40690CB00017B/3470